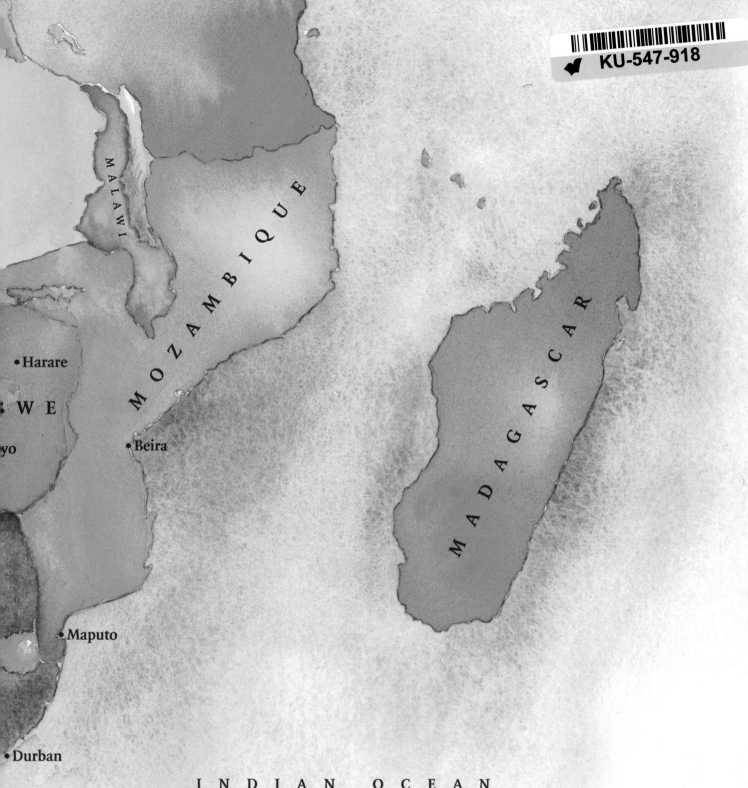

MALAWI

MOZAMBIQUE

MADAGASCAR

• Harare

WE

yo

• Beira

• Maputo

• Durban

INDIAN OCEAN

ON THE TRAIL OF
THE WILD

ON THE TRAIL OF
THE WILD

Encounters in the Southern African Bush

Text and Photography
Raphael Ben-Shahar

Frontispiece:
Bull elephant at camp.

Endpaper: Map of Africa

© 1999 Könemann Verlagsgesellschaft mbH
Bonner Straße 126, D – 50968 Cologne

Art Direction and Project Coordination: Peter Feierabend
Project Manager: Bettina Kaufmann
Assistant: Alex Morkramer
Editor: Donald Reid, Edinburgh
Layout: Samantha Finn, Mark Thomson, International Design UK Ltd., London
Maps: International Design UK Ltd., London
Production Manager: Detlev Schaper
Production: Mark Voges
Reproduction: CDN, Caselle di Sommacampacna and divis GmbH, Cologne
Printing and Binding: Imprimerie Jean Lamour, Maxéville

Printed in France

ISBN 3-8290-1446-5
10 9 8 7 6 5 4 3 2 1

The elephants veered and spread like a fan. It was a large herd, 14 females with their young and four bulls. I knew what was coming. There was no mistake. They were going to attack me.

Introduction

Years of observing elephants in the wild had taught me that nothing stops a charging herd, not even rapid machine gun fire. Now I was in the wrong place at the wrong time. A strange kind of calmness enveloped the bush as the elephants rushed silently and closed the distance between us. Seconds ago the herd had been idly standing around flapping their ears surrounded by the serene atmosphere that only the African bush possesses. Now two of the bulls were advancing ahead of the raging herd. The nearest camp wasn't far away, but it was no refuge. I could not turn my back and run away. Impact was imminent.

Up until that moment, my life in the bush had been filled with the harmony and beauty of nature. Observing intimately the lives of animals, being close to them and understanding the ways of the bush was to me the essence of being in Africa. I had even sensed a secret understanding developing between the animals and myself – I was not to disturb them and they, in turn, would open up their worlds to me. And I had come to know them all, from the smallest insect to the largest animal, the elephant. Together, they formed the intricate web of life that makes the bush so compelling.

It all began for me when I went with my father on a safari to Kenya and Tanzania. I was a small boy, filled with curiosity and eager to find out all about the bush. Thirty years later, I can still vividly remember the overhanging mist on the slopes of the Ngorongoro as we drove down into the crater. I can recall being inside the minivan (or 'Kombi,' as everyone there called it) for many hours each day, my car-sickness intensified by the gusts of dust and petrol fumes that enveloped us from time to time. When we suffered a puncture on an isolated track in the Lake Manyara National Park in Tanzania I got out and sat down on a nearby fallen log. The air was moist and cool. Dung beetles buzzed as they flew to freshly deposited dung piles. Then I heard the sound of branches crunching, and I realized that a herd of elephants was browsing nearby. I could vaguely make out their black shapes against the evergreen forest that dropped down from the escarpment, and became aware that other ele-

phants were closer, more heard than observed. Not far away from the elephants, a troop of baboons was busy grooming and playing. Some sat on fallen logs and a termite mound, overlooking the scene and basking their bodies in the sparse sun rays that penetrated the low cloud. It looked like a scene out of heaven, a dream. If someone had told me then that I would find my way back to the bush sometime, I would not have been surprised.

For many years after, the East African experience remained dormant, like a glowing fire, waiting for the right moment to burst into flames. When I enrolled at the university, it seemed a natural choice for me to study biology as an undergraduate. During my time off from the long hours of books and lectures, I worked in a zoo. I remember sitting on the ledge of the elephants' enclosure watching a trail of ants, and wondering about the ways each creature perceived its world. They were so different, the ant and the elephant, so far apart on the scale of things, yet they lived together in the zoo and in nature. The intelligence, confidence and complexity of the elephants were obvious. Yet as the ants touched each other with their antennae, they were sending invisible chemical substances to the other members of their colony. I figured that the communication between ants also involved a certain body language just like the elephants, which often touched one another with their trunks and sent inaudible messages about their moods and intentions. I wondered what they were thinking about. What is the world like in the mind of an ant? Or an elephant?

During the course of my studies I realized that although there was a holistic concept of small and large creatures comprising a delicate network at the heart of a viable ecosystem, the interactions between them were poorly understood. Moreover, many of the articles I read about the African wilderness were already emphasizing the role of man in the destruction of natural areas. Alarming reports described the massive elephant mortality in East Africa, first as a result of a drought, then as poachers in their quest for ivory destroyed hundreds more. At first, I had marveled how animals adjusted to living in close quarters with people. I decided that if there was a way to link development with the viability of natural systems that might be the right purpose for fulfilling my long-nurtured ambition to return to Africa.

Professor John Skinner of the Mammal Research Institute at the University of Pretoria offered me a place on his B.Sc. honors course. He indicated that I could utilize the degree as a precursor to an M.Sc., which offered me a great opportunity to come to grips with the African wilderness.

Not long after arriving in South Africa, I made the long trip to Namibia with some classmates, and made inquiries about the possibility of conducting fieldwork in Etosha National Park in the northern part of the country. I had already heard much about the reserve and its wildlife. The harsh and desolate environment contrasted with the vitality of its teeming wildlife and provided fuel for my thoughts about the connections between wildlife and their habitats. How can a bleak and harsh landscape provide for a plethora of wildlife? What is the secret of their survival?

Etosha is situated in a marginal area, threatened by the encroachment of the desert in the west. In the past, there had been little human intervention because much of Etosha's land is unsuitable for agriculture and livestock husbandry. Taking these facts together, I wondered whether they suggested that the congregation of wildlife was artificial. It seemed as if the areas allocated to serve as sanctuaries were marginal areas both for livestock and wildlife.

Some of the answers to these questions were revealed during the course of my studies and further trips to Namibia, although the project I was hoping to take part in there was canceled. But as one door closed, another opened. After several months, I set off to Lapalala Wilderness, a remote nature reserve situated in the Northern Province of South Africa. I was to follow roan antelope that had recently been introduced to their former range from a provincial nature reserve. Previously, the roan had been in small, well-managed reserves where they did not suffer predator pressure and were well taken care of. Rangers would feed the animals at times of drought and food shortage, and even provide veterinary treatment. Some of the animals released into Lapalala had radio collars attached, and I was to record how they interacted with their new environment.

The ranger took me on a tour of the reserve, which is situated in an area of high plateau cut by deep ravines. Even by the time of my arrival, one radio-collared animal had died and the transmitter on another was sending back only weak signals. Over a crackling phone line, I explained the situation to Professor Skinner. He ordered me back to Pretoria and the project was promptly canceled.

However, I felt it might be possible to broaden the scope of my research in the Waterberg to include other antelope species beyond the roan, such as the rare sable and the tsessebe, and complete a study on their habitat preferences in the area with a view to their future conservation. Even at this early stage, I understood that in order to conserve just one species, a thorough knowledge of the composite interactions that take place in an ecosystem, starting with the soils and moving through plants and animals, is vital. A month later, I was settling into a shack on a prominent hill in Lapalala Wilderness.

White rhinos can be found in groups that typically comprise a female and her offspring.

I have to confess that I didn't much like my first bush experience. Here I was, completely isolated, with no means of transport but my legs. Worse than that, I was conducting my study on an introduced species in a former cattle ranch. I found myself in a makeshift zoo in the middle of nowhere. This was a long way from the romantic dreams I had about the African bush where I would wake up to see an elephant browsing on the creeper in the porch or lie on my bed at night and listen to the distant roar of lions.

Yet, Africa was there, vibrant, on smaller scales. For almost a year, I walked the area daily, sampling soils and vegetation and marking the location of animals I spotted. I examined the grasses, insects, and lizards. I learned to listen to the sounds of birds and got to know each species by its call. I became familiar with the spoor of the different animal tracks and with the help of a game scout, Andreas, not only did my Afrikaans improve, but also my ability to search for animals. Andreas was a fine field man who had a special sensitivity to the bush. While we were walking together, things that would go unnoticed by me, such as a broken twig or a small depression on the ground, meant an entire world to him. Here was the territory marking of a bushbuck, there was the tiny trap of an ant lion in the soft sand. With great patience, Andreas explained the ways of the bush to me. Amongst the grasses, insects, trees, and roan, there was logic imbedded. I could touch it, sometimes explain bits, but never quite understand how it all fitted together. Yet my research has shown me that the roan was not coping well with the rugged terrain and the type of grasses that were growing in the Waterberg, and at the conclusion of my thesis I was able to make some recommendations. Even if these were neither very revealing, nor optimistic, they were facts that the local managers could build upon for the future conservation of the area. For my part, however, my appetite for the mysteries of the bush and its spellbound surroundings had only intensified.

After this, a Ph.D. seemed the best way for me to pursue my search for the answers entombed in the wilderness. Through a friend I had met while researching in Lapalala, I got in touch with the directors of Sabi-Sabi, a private game reserve in the eastern part of South Africa. Sabi-Sabi is part of a large consortium of private reserves called the Sabi-Sand; together, the reserves in the Sabi-Sand constituted the core of upper-market wildlife tourism in South Africa. Relying on the vast pool of nature in the Kruger National Park, the Sabi-Sand was expected to maintain high species diversity and the natural rhythm of life. But was it really natural? Past human intervention had left its scars on the land, and the gently undulating terrain, covered with plumes of grassland and bush, was gutted with pale veins of eroded land. It was believed that the damaged habitats reduced the potential sustainable capacity of the land and made game scarcer. Some reserves within the Sabi-Sand conglomerate had already begun rehabilitating these habitats, but somehow it seemed to me that many of their methods were excessive and would not achieve the objective of the recovery of game in the Sabi-Sand. Hence, my main question was, what exactly are the factors that influence the sustainable capacity of the land for large herbivorous species like the impala, zebra and wildebeest?

During my time in the reserve, I became attached to its rhythms. I explored the area with a battered Landrover and on foot and cemented the principles I had learned at Lapalala by starting first to look at the small and seemingly insignificant aspects. The geological formations of the area and soil types played a major role in my thesis, while aspects such as rainfall were also very important in this semi-arid environment. The water that percolated beneath ground level flowed in peculiar patterns and the accumulation of moisture at different depths affected the growth patterns of plants. I investigated the composition of plants and discovered what the large herbivores were eating. My walks allowed me fascinating observations on the small creatures of the bush, and sometimes brought a few encounters with larger wildlife. Yet I was beginning to see a certain vague order in the makeshift of the bush. I started to learn the habits of the lions and leopards that hung around in the vicinity of the lodge, and developed an unspoken dialogue with them. They allowed me to stay at close quarters provided I did not disturb their ways of life. Toward the end of my time in the Sabi-Sand, I knew where and when to go to find the most thrilling of these carnivore's activities. While the lions and leopards slept, I worked on my thesis. As the sun was about to set, I would drive out and follow them while they captured prey, fought with hyenas and had their cubs. When the activity died down, I retired to my room in anticipation of the coming dawn.

After Sabi-Sabi I headed to Oxford University for my post-doctoral study. Shortly before I left South Africa, however, I had a chance to attend a symposium of the Southern African Zoological Society at Etosha. In the breaks between lectures, and in between photographing elephant bulls at the Okaukuejo waterhole that borders the camp, one speaker indicated that the

Department of Wildlife would welcome a study on the interactions of elephants and their habitats. I left Etosha with great expectations for a new project.

A year later I was back in Africa cruising in a brand new Landrover along the road that connects Gaborone, the capital of Botswana, with Kasane, a northern border town. No longer was I in a small reserve where you could drive a scrap vehicle and if necessary walk to the workshop for replacement parts. This time, a working vehicle could be the difference between life and death. The timing of my project (1990) was also important as different organizations were gearing up for a forthcoming CITES (Convention of International Trade in Endangered Species) meeting about the fate of elephants and the future status of the ivory trade. Delegates wanted to back their arguments with robust data. Nobody really knew about the situation in northern Botswana except for the commonly held notion that elephants were causing havoc along the riverine woodlands. Many scientists speculated that the damage would spread inland as the elephant population grew. At that time the northern Botswana elephant herd was the largest in Africa, totaling some 50,000.

One was keen to show that the elephants were a principal factor in the destruction of woodland in northern Botswana and that elephant culling was therefore necessary for the maintenance of a viable ecosystem. I suspected that there were other interests involved in such a determined line of approach. By then, I felt I was a seasoned field researcher and that I knew my way around savanna ecosystems. It was a plain matter of measuring and recording and allowing the numbers to tell their tale. From the beginning, it was obvious that elephants were only one factor that affected the vegetation. Like before, I emphasized the small and seemly insignificant components. As it turned out, drought, fire, flooding, plant disease and other herbivores also had a considerable role in shaping northern Botswana's web of life, affecting the survival of woodlands. Not wanting to compromise my academic integrity, I gave up the Landrover that I had grown so found of and also the promised funding. Fortunately, I was still able to continue with the project and my bitterness was forgotten once I secured alternative funding. Again, I was back out there, inhaling deep the air of freedom.

For nearly three years I stayed in Savuti, at the heart of Chobe National Park. Life there was a stark contrast to the style of Sabi-Sabi, and my tented camp in the middle of nowhere was a far cry from the luxurious lodge. I had to cope with a harsh environment full of extremes. For days, I used to work in complete isolation in the bush. The exhilarating sense of freedom was sometimes replaced by the creeping anxiety that I was lost. Lines drawn on even the most detailed maps available represented an approximation to what was supposed to be on the ground. And often, the best way of getting to a remote spot was to drive on a compass bearing. But the more I became familiar with the region, the more the desolate sites took on a reassuring and familiar feel. When I returned to camp, it was teeming with life. When there were no human guests, animals such as lions, elephants and leopards were frequent visitors. Sharing a living took on a different dimension.

By the third year of my stay at Savuti, however, the bush had beset me. My sense of purpose diminished. The capacity of land to carry elephants crystalized in terms of concepts and numbers. I was able to calculate how many elephants could be sustained in specific habitats under certain conditions without causing the local woodland to deteriorate. As much as the natural elements had control over the number of elephants that northern Botswana can carry, man also had a say.

Then came the attack. Maybe the timing wasn't coincidental. My devotion to the research had dissipated and I had lost my direction. Miraculously, I survived the attack – not many people have seen the rage of a large elephant herd out in the open and lived to recall it. After a frustrating and prolonged period of medical treatment that took nearly two years, I came back to the bush. It was my mistake that had prompted the attack, as by unwittingly cornering the elephants I had broken the rules of understanding that I had with the animals. Yet the attack confirmed the existence of such rules, albeit in a very profound way.

When you walk in the African bush, it can seem as if nothing much is happening. Yet if you look around more closely, bend to the ground or listen for subtle sounds, an entire world will open before you. Suddenly, you realize that the bush is teeming with life and vitality. There is an incredible diversity of life forms and the richness of life and pungent realities inspire a sensual pureness that cannot and should not be ignored. Whenever I stay there and meet other people who have a similar understanding, we share a bond, created and intensified by the bush. This is the main motivation for this book. I have brought together here a small collection of impressions gathered from the African bush in the hope that they will inspire you to come and share the same feeling. For me, my heart will always be in the African bush, and the savannas will always be there, waiting, beckoning.

Namibian Mirages – Etosha and the Namib Desert

There is something in the Namibian landscape that makes its barren and sun-baked deserts irresistible. For anyone who envisages typical African savannas as lush grasslands stretching beyond the horizon, Namibia is very different. Its animals, that seem so out of place, merely confirm the surreal nature of the landscape. Giraffes and elephants that are typically seen elsewhere browsing on acacia trees, immersed in a sea of bush and grasslands, stand out in the desert among the swirling, simmering heat waves. Yet some creatures, like the small beetles that struggle up sandy dunes against wind-driven showers of sand grains, seem to be uniquely and naturally at home in this harsh environment.

Typically, the struggle for survival for all animal species revolves around finding food and successfully raising offspring. In the desert environment, coping with the extreme temperature range and the scarcity of moisture only make it even tougher. In fact, it is the insects and reptiles that are the true rulers of the desert, having the ability not only to extract fluids from their food, but also to minimize water loss from their bodies. Birds and mammals exploit their opportunities, albeit brief, when the desert offers favorable conditions for finding food and breeding. One example of this is found west of the Namib Desert where the blue hues of the Atlantic Ocean contrast with the pale

ANGOLA

• Oshakati

ETOSHA
NATIONAL PARK

NAMIBIA

SKELETON
COAST
NATIONAL
PARK

• Otjiwarongo

BOTSWANA

Namib Desert

• Windhoek

Olifants River

Nossob River

ATLANTIC OCEAN

• Lüderitz

• Keetmanshoop

SOUTH
AFRICA

sand dunes and red sandstone rocks on the shore. Here, a variety of animals such as sea birds and seals establish breeding colonies each year in a peculiar display of contempt against the harsh environment.

I knew about this harshness before coming to Namibia, yet I was irresistibly drawn to the expansive landscape that seems to inspire a feeling of freedom. In this lightly populated land, wind and sand dominate life and the struggle for survival. I was intrigued to find out how animals coped with the harsh environment. In particular, I was interested in the marginal transition areas between deserts and the moister habitats of semi-arid savannas. The surroundings of Etosha National Park perhaps epitomize the endless struggle between the creeping desert and the grassland and bush, that attract wildlife. Herds of zebra and wildebeest migrate over large distances and mingle with springbok and the local oryx species, the gemsbok, in the search for a new flush of green grass. Many of the bird species are ground dwellers, such as the korhaans which are always searching for insects between the pebbles and rocks. Surface water is scarce and the few waterholes are the hubs of the diurnal movements of game, particularly during the dry season. Sitting close to the edge of a waterhole offers incredible opportunities to witness the intimate lives of animals in the bush.

As I followed animals across the Namibian landscape with a camera and notepad, days went by unnoticed and time lost its meaning. I gradually came to know the elusive elements of animals' lives and I was left with a yearning to stay longer, to capture more of this beauty on film.

Etosha

This unique wildlife sanctuary is among the largest national parks in Africa. It extends over an area of 22,270 square kilometers, of which the large salt pan in the middle takes up about a third. One of the unique features of Etosha is the abundance and diversity of game species normally found in tropic savanna environments that venture to the edge of the desert. Here, set against the white, calcareous landscape, many of the common savanna species are found, except for water-dependent species such as buffalo and hippopotamus. Yet, by comparison to the productive savanna areas in East and southern Africa, the eastern and central parts of Etosha receive meager amounts of rainfall. Springbok and gemsbok, which are better adapted to arid conditions, can cope with the relative paucity of nutritional fodder, but the threat of prolonged drought hangs like a dark cloud over animals such as wildebeest and zebra. All the herbivores, however, have the capacity to migrate over large distances and are constantly searching for greener pastures.

In the local Ovambo dialect, Etosha means "the place of dry water." There is a prolonged dry and hot season from October until the onset of the rains, late in December. The rains come in the form of thunderstorms, and, as a consequence, the distribution of rain is patchy. The rapid changes in weather conditions bring about dramatic changes to the life styles of animals in Etosha, especially in years when the reserve receives a higher rainfall and the baked ground of the pan becomes covered with water.

Artesian springs flow throughout the year on the southern edge of the pan. The water from the highlands that border the southern part of Etosha, where rainfall is greater, is carried on impermeable shallow bedrock created from the sedimentation of an ancient lake. A year of average rainfall is sufficient for water to reach the pan, but to distribute the pressure of grazing throughout the reserve, and add tourist attraction sites, the Nature Conservation and Tourism Division of the Namibian Government has provided additional artificial water sources. These waterholes are mostly situated around the edge of the pan and pass water to a trough by pumps powered by solar panels.

Elephants, giraffes, kudus and gemsbok are among the more prominent animals that frequent the waterholes. The gemsbok is one of a group of four species of oryx that are distributed throughout arid areas in Africa and the Arabic peninsula. Etosha is a typical gemsbok habitat and the waterholes often see confrontations between territorial males. The onset of the rains is the cue for ungulates to abandon the waterholes. Soon after, the desolate landscape of the arid

Opposite:
African moringa trees form a dense stand west of the Etosha Pan. The peculiar shape of the tree and its bark led to the naming of the area, which is called "the enchanted forest."

Wildebeest at the edge of the Etosha Pan.

west is covered by grass and well-trodden tracks radiate from the waterholes and disappear into the open plains and thick bush. The elephant population of Etosha disperses to the mopane woodlands in the south. Grasses that grow in the woodlands supplement their diet and the elephants will remain there as long as water and nutritious food are available.

Etosha is well known for its prominent population of carnivores. The plains on the edge of the pan offer visitors uninterrupted views and a good opportunity to see a pride of lions, hyenas or even a solitary leopard. Predators can also be observed at close quarters near the water holes. Towards the peak of the dry season, the frequency of visits by large herbivores to waterholes increases, and a lion ambush is not an uncommon sight.

Biologists, however, have monitored with concern the gradual decline in the number of wildebeest in the reserve. Over a span of only a few years, the wildebeest population declined from 10,000 when the reserve was first fenced, to its present level of a few thousand. A similar trend was observed with the zebra population although the decline has not been as dramatic. Preliminary research indicated that lions were the probable cause for the demise of the wildebeest and zebra populations. Accordingly, researchers suggested a limit to the number of animals in the reserve. Lions were followed on an annual basis throughout Etosha, and considerable effort was put into identifying indi-

vidual members of prides and the make-up of family trees within different prides. Under the auspices of a competent veterinary team, dozens of lions were tranquilized, measured and marked for future identification. Radio collars were attached to the senior members of some prides and a preliminary attempt was made at birth control for lionesses. Capsules that release hormones were implanted under the skin of lionesses in prides where the number of lions was high. However, the research was only partially successful. Although a decline in birth rates was observed among the treated lionesses, these prides suffered from an increase in turnover rates and their structure became rather unstable. In addition, from the beginning of the lion research in Etosha, a prolonged drought had affected the region, and a further decline in the number of large herbivores occurred. Subsequently, the lion population also suffered a dramatic decline. With the onset of rains, it was expected that the numbers of herbivores and lions would recover to their former levels, but this did not occur and it soon became evident that lions were not the primary cause of the decline in large herbivores.

Shortly after its proclamation in the mid-1950s, Etosha was surrounded by a game-proof fence reinforced with steel cables. The effect of this was to isolate the populations of large herbivores and prevent them from reaching vital resources, particularly the Okavango River and its adjoining flood plains to the

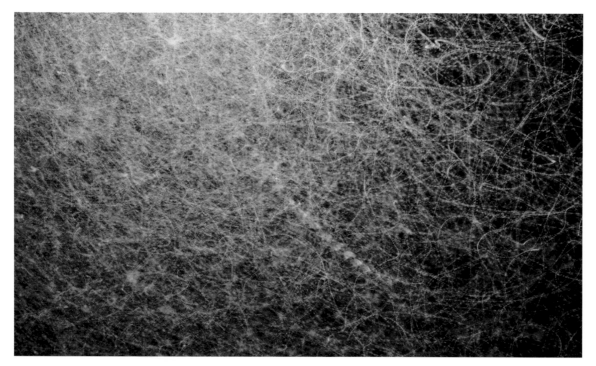

Swarms of moths at night during the wet season. The insects were photographed using a long exposure. The lines show the flight path of the insects, while the small "blips" represent the flutter of wings.

Localized rainfall patterns in the desert mean a nomadic lifestyle for its large herbivorous residents.

Drops of acacia resin accumulate on the pod of the acacia tree. Many herbivores enjoy the taste of the resin, while ants may utilize its sugar contents. In return, the ants protect the acacia from herbivores by clinging to it in a large column and biting ferociously at any browsers.

The Popa Falls of the Okavango River in the Caprivi Strip is the only place before the Angolan Highlands where there are rapids. The area of the rapids is safe for bathers because hippos seldom venture to shallow water during the day where they are exposed to the scorching rays of the sun.

Right:
A local carrying fire wood on her head. The weight of the load can easily reach 50 kilograms.

Opposite:
Watch out for elephants! This sign in the Caprivi Strip, a favorite elephant crossing point in the dry season, warns drivers about elephants crossing the road on their way to drink from the Zambezi.

Following pages:
A camel thorn acacia under a sand storm.

north of Etosha. Until less than a century ago, before human settlement had encroached into the area, wildlife had uninterrupted access to the water and the habitats around the river. This means that in its current condition, and in spite of its large size, Etosha can carry only a limited number of herbivores that have to make do with the resources available within the boundaries of the park. It is thus unlikely that there will be a significant recovery in the numbers of large herbivores even in good rainfall years, unless the animals can regain access to their former range.

Camel thorn

Widespread in the arid regions of southern Africa, the camel thorn tree derives its name not from the camel, but from a direct translation of the Afrikaans "Kameeldoring," meaning the acacia of the giraffe. A deciduous tree that looses its leaves for a short period only, its thorns are long and hard and its roots penetrate deep into sandy soils. One of the characteristics of camel thorn woodland is the occurrence of even age groups. This means that within a certain area, most camel thorn trees have similar heights and crown development. This phenomenon is linked to patterns of rainfall. Even in areas where the soil contains rich acacia seed banks, the development and establishment of large numbers of seedlings is confined to years when there is sufficient rainfall.

The camel thorn is among the first tree species in the bush to leaf in the early spring and thus provides browse at a critical time of the year, when other food sources have dwindled. The pods are also a viable food source for animals because of their high nutritional value and high phosphorous contents. Typically, a mature elephant bull will approach the trunk of a camel thorn and lean against it, shaking the tree for several seconds. Ripe pods fall to the ground, and are picked up one by one by the elephant using its trunk. Camel thorn trees are do not live for long periods, having a life expectancy of only 100 to 150 years. The trees are also highly susceptible to the effects of flooding, as sudden rises in the water table can suffocate the roots and kill the tree.

Mopane worms

Elephants that head south from Etosha in search of the mopane woodlands may find themselves competing for this favorite food source with a slightly surprising rival, caterpillars. The caterpillars, the larval stage of the mopane moth, emerge in their thousands in the rainy season and feed entirely on mopane leaves. In large numbers, the caterpillars can reduce significantly, if not deplete, this food source for elephants. However, the numbers of caterpillars are limited by their food sources. Even the caterpillars may migrate in large columns in search of an alternative supply of mopane, if food is scarce. Interestingly, mopane caterpillars are a sought-after delicacy among the local people.

Left:
A sand storm engulfs trees and shrubs.

Opposite:
Black rhino are not a common sight in Etosha National Park, although the park is still considered one of its refuges and strongholds.

Elephant bulls at the Okaukuejo waterhole in Etosha National Park. The elephant population in the park, although relatively small, is a major tourist attraction.

Goliath frog

The Goliath frog is another example of the opportunistic nature of survival strategies in arid regions. The largest frog in Africa, it remains dormant in crusted mud during the dry season. The delicate membranes that envelop the frog maintain the frog's vital functions until rain percolates through to the buried frogs. The water dissolves the membranes and provides the cue for the emergence of the frog and the beginning of their reproductive cycle. Thousands of frogs mate and lay thereafter millions of eggs. Of the vast number of tadpoles which hatch and develop in the puddles only a few survive because they provide a rich food source for a multitude of water birds.

Red-Billed quelea

The quelea is a member of the weaver family. During the dry season, thousands of queleas flock together and migrate to the semi-arid areas of southern Africa. Early in the spring, before the first rains, queleas make their nests on branches of trees before the cloak of new leaves appears. The male is responsible for building the nest, but as soon as this is done mating takes place, without preliminary courtship displays. The first egg is laid by the end of the following day. The pair share the incubation of eggs for two weeks.

The young hatch at approximately the same time, littering the ground with egg shells. The reproductive potential of the quelea is enormous and no matter how many predators are attracted to the quelea colonies, their reproduction potential overwhelms the predation pressure. A fast maturation rate means the young reach sexual maturity by the end of their first year. The quelea is notorious for the damage it can cause to crops, and migration tends to be the consequence of a local shortage in food.

Black korhaan

A member of the bustard family, the black korhaan is found across the arid regions of southern Africa. In addition to its black color, this korhaan is conspicuous because of its shrieking. While males will choose prominent spots, such as the top of termite mounds, to stand, females are elusive. During courting displays, the male will fly up, hover, and slowly descend with wings fluttering, calling continuously and loudly. Displaying males are quite noisy, giving a harsh "keorak-keorak-keorak-keorak" call.

Opposite:
A black korhaan cleans and arranges its feathers.

A male black korhaan attentively observing its territory in Etosha National Park.

Bustards

The Kori bustard belongs to a family that is well represented in southern Africa. It is a common resident of dry, long-grass savanna areas on the fringes of arid zones. They are fairly large birds with long legs but only three toes. Although their coloration is subdued, particularly on the upper parts, their calls are conspicuous. Being so tall, the Kori bustard is able to spot enemies from a long distance away, and on the approach of an enemy it will stride away rapidly. If danger is imminent, it will take off reluctantly after a short run. The flight of the Kori bustard is short and heavy. Nonetheless, it is a migratory species, when it moves to avoid adverse conditions in deserts and their consequent shortages of food. It feeds on carrion, seeds, insects and small mammals and reptiles. Bee eaters are often seen sitting on the back of the Kori bustard while foraging for flying insects.

While many bird species are able, thanks to their natural mobility, to avoid the hostile desert climate, other species are true desert dwellers and live in the desert year round. Some birds like eagles and vultures will escape the soaring heat by gliding at great heights utilizing thermal air currents, while others have less developed wings that require them to adapt to hot conditions. Having no efficient heat-exchanging mechanisms such as sweat glands, desert-dwelling birds vaporize water through their lungs to regulate body temperature.

In cold temperatures, they erect their feathers and create air pockets that insulate the body from the cold weather. However, in hot temperatures, the feathers are quite useless, and birds have to rely on their relatively high body temperature to minimize their need for water. Many can subsist on fluids derived from the plants, insects, mammals or other birds that they eat. Some bird species also excrete very concentrated urine and can utilize their salt glands to minimize water loss.

Wahlberg's eagle

This small eagle is commonly found in moist scrub and woodland savannas. Wahlberg's eagles return to the same nest each year, and are often seen perched on tall trees scanning their surroundings. The bird's favorite prey items include small rodents, birds, reptiles and insects, particularly termites.

Opposite:
A steppe eagle on the lookout for prey as a flock of red-billed quelea flies past.

A couple of Kori bustards at the edge of Etosha Pan. The Kori bustard is a heavy bird that prefers to outrun its quarry than take to the air.

A Wahlberg's eagle tightens its grip on the remains of a small antelope.

Ostrich

By far the most conspicuous bird on the African savannas, an ostrich can weigh well above 100 kilograms and reach up to two meters in height. They are flightless, but can reach the speed of 70 kilometers per hour without pulling extra effort. They feed on plants, succulents, seeds and berries, and will swallow hard objects such as stones and pebbles to assist the crushing of hard parts of plants in their stomach.

Ostriches associate in pairs and are found in small scattered parties as well as singly. Monogamous pairs are the rule although males may be polygamous. They nest on the ground, and if more than one female accompanies the male, they will both lay eggs in the same hollow scrape on the ground. As a result, nests can include a large number of eggs. The male may incubate the eggs at night and the female during the day. There is a hierarchy among females, as low-ranked females will have their eggs pushed to the edge of the nest by the dominant female. It is not clear, however, how the dominant female recognizes her own eggs. Eggs pushed to the periphery of the nest receive less attention and may remain exposed to the sun to the point where the egg will become infertile. In addition, eggs on the periphery are also exposed to trampling by a fellow ostrich as well as to predation by jackals. Although the shell is hardened, carnivores can crush the eggs and jackals will push and throw eggs against solid objects in order to break them.

Living in arid areas, ostrich minimize water loss largely through behavioral thermo-regulation. When faced with high intensity solar radiation and high ambient temperatures, ostriches turn toward the sun and move their wings down and away from the thorax. Being exposed and naked, the thorax functions as a thermal window for the body, facilitating radiant and convective heat loss. In addition, erect dorsal feathers expose a further section of the skin to the movement of outside air. In this way, the ostrich maximizes convective cooling if the ambient temperature is below the temperature of the body (40°C). At night, however, ostrich (along with other creatures of the desert) are faced with an opposite problem. To conserve heat in the cold nights, they fold their wings close to the thorax and tuck their naked legs beneath themselves as they huddle close to the ground. In addition, they are able to lower their metabolic rates. This adaptation is supplemented by the reduction of water loss through the urine. The ostrich secretes uric acid along with mucus that facilitates the extraction. The mucus is secreted from special cells and appears in the form of a white paste.

Like many other desert animals, the activity of ostriches is finely tuned to the change of ambient temperature. This group is exercising in the morning near the Etosha Pan.

Ground squirrels are social rodents that retain close ties among group members.

Ground squirrel

The ground squirrel is a typical dweller of arid savannas, although its habitat is confined to the western parts of southern Africa. It prefers open areas with sparse vegetation cover and a hard surface, and is mostly found on the fringes of dry watercourses, flood plains and overgrazed areas. It avoids loose sandy areas, and hence is absent from the dunes of the Namib Desert. Ground squirrels live in colonies, and in nature reserves they will often dig their burrows close to and underneath roads. These burrows provide superb insulation against the heat and minimize temperature fluctuations to range between 11 and 14 °C.

The squirrels have sharp claws and massive incisors that, similar to other rodents, grow throughout their lives, and which they use to dig their tunnel systems. These have many entrances, expanding in some areas while other parts become disused and entrances are closed by the occupants. Females and their offspring constitute the core of a ground squirrel

colony, as adult males do not remain constantly with the group. Instead, males move around between groups and remain for several weeks with a group where the females are in estrus. There is no particular breeding peak and females have one litter per year. The young are born altricial – blind, naked and requiring care.

Ground squirrels are diurnal, becoming active only in the late morning when the sun has already warmed the ground. Activity ceases before sunset. On emerging from their burrows in the morning, they will mark their territory by scraping a small hole near the burrow, then urinating or pressing their anus into the depression, or by rubbing their snouts against nearby stones. The squirrels will then bask in the sun, stretching their limbs and exposing their bellies. On very hot days, they will perform similar activities in the shade.

Frequently, ground squirrels share their burrow system with members of the mongoose family. This may be a form of anti-predator protection, as the small carnivores and the rodent share mutual enemies. They appear to live in harmony and sun themselves close to one another, although the yellow mongoose is known to eat sick or injured ground squirrels.

Ground squirrels are predominantly vegetarian, feeding on grass leaves and stems, seeds, bulbs and roots, although their diet also includes a small amount of insects. The squirrels will dig for bulbs and plant roots and may pull down the stems of grasses and low shrubs to reach leaves.

Yellow mongoose

A common resident of arid savannas in the southern African region, the yellow mongoose is mostly diurnal and lives either in colonies, smaller family units or in pairs. Mongooses will either expand existing springhare burrows or dig their own tunnels, although they do sometimes share burrows with other species, particularly suricates and ground squirrels.

Each colony consists of a breeding pair and their offspring. Mature mongooses may associate with the colony but live separately in nearby burrows. A clear hierarchy exists whereby even younger animals may dominate old adults. The alpha male demarcates and defends its territory, and is sometimes assisted by the alpha female.

Living in arid conditions, the yellow mongoose modifies its daily activity patterns according to the conditions. In the hot summer, foraging activity is confined to the first hours after sunrise, after which it will rest in the shade of shrubs near its burrows. It resumes foraging in late afternoon and retires shortly before dark. On cold winter mornings, the mongooses will emerge briefly at sunrise to urinate, then retreat and appear again late in the morning when it is warmer. Foraging activity only starts after a considerable time has been spent sunbathing.

Colony members forage individually but maintain mutual contact. The alpha male devotes a considerable amount of time to territory marking, and males will seldom venture beyond these boundaries. Living in open areas, visual communication is also important. Yellow mongooses can rear on their hind legs to look out for approaching danger. The mongoose's long tail is also used to convey information, for example, a raised and curved tail indicates alarm.

Black-backed jackal

Another common resident of southern African savannas, the black-backed jackal is seen at carcasses alongside vultures and hyenas, although it does not restrict itself to eating carrion. Highly opportunistic, it will take insects, rodents, small hares, lizards and concealed antelope fawns, as well as fruits and berries.

Black-backed jackals associate in monogamous pairs and maintain a territory. Their success in raising a litter depends on the amount of assistance the parents receive from helpers. These helpers, typically

A yellow mongoose rears up while foraging, to observe the approach of predators.

yearlings of previous litters, spend much time near the den and will bring food to the young, keep a watchful eye over them and warn of any approaching danger. As they mature, black-backed jackals tend to establish a strict ranking order. The order of dominance between cubs may determine which remains and which leaves the group. Dominant cubs receive a greater share of the food brought to the den, and show better foraging capabilities, and so would be the likely candidates to leave and form their own independent group. But, should conditions be adverse, dominant cubs may force subordinates to move away. The activities of the parents are closely coordinated and include territory marking and defense, hunting, sharing food and providing for their offspring.

At a carcass, jackals have remarkable boldness and will grab pieces of it while lions and hyenas are feeding at the site. Like many other dog-like animals, jackals may cache surplus meat, burying it near a prominent land mark. Most caches are retrieved within a day, although hyenas may rob some.

Jackals represent an important part in the food chain in Etosha, although not always for the benefit of other animals. When access roads in Etosha were constructed to increase the opportunity for tourists to view wildlife without causing too much disturbance to the environment, small quarries were dug to provide gravel for the roads. Unfortunately, as rain water gathered in these small pans they proved ideal conditions for the bacteria that spread anthrax to flourish. When animals came to drink from these pools, the bacteria would invade their body through a small cut or mouth sore. Ultimately, after profuse hemorrhaging, the animals die, and the anthrax spread quickly through the natural food chains as vultures, jackals and hyenas, which are immune to anthrax, would pollute further water sources by drinking in them after eating a contaminated carcass. When the dire effect of the gravel

A black-backed jackal examines a carcass it has just encountered.

quarries was discovered, different gravel from outside the reserve was brought in to pave the roads and cover the artificial depressions. Anthrax, however, is now endemic to the area, and in an effort to eradicate the disease, animal carcasses are buried and covered with rocks in the hope that scavengers will not find them.

Damara dik-dik

The smallest antelope in Africa, the Damara dik-dik weighs up to six kilograms. It prefers dense vegetation cover with an ample diversity of browse species, although the Damara dik-dik of southern Africa is associated with habitats with sparse grass. Thus areas that have suffered from overgrazing of game and livestock, such as Etosha National Park and its neighboring farms, are particularly suitable.

To survive the heat in arid regions like Namibia, a dik-dik cools the blood in its nasal passages. Its extended snout means that the nasal vestibule, and hence the area of moist skin available for evaporative cooling, is enlarged. While panting, the dik-dik conserves energy by reducing the blood flow to its muscles, except those involved in breathing.

The Damara dik-dik feeds on a wide range of the plants within its reach, although its small, delicate mouth is highly selective about the parts of plants it feeds on. It may nibble the tips of young grass shoots, but otherwise will refrain from grazing. Damara dik-dik are active during the day, although activity is largely determined by the ambient temperature. As such, in hot weather, they become nocturnal and rest in the shade during the day.

Damara dik-diks live in monogamous pairs and are territorial. The male is dominant and will defend its territory against intruders. The size of territory is determined by the availability of plant food during the dry season and the availability of shelter. Male offspring are forced by their father to leave on reaching adolescence, but soon thereafter the young dik-diks are able to establish pair bonds and territories, even though they are not fully mature.

Because of their small size, Damara dik-diks are vulnerable to a large number of predators. At a hint of danger, the dik-dik freezes. Gradually, males will move their head in an attempt to verify the source of the danger while the female remains motionless. Depending on the source of danger, the dik-dik then explodes in a zigzag run and freezes under a new cover.

Steenbok

The steenbok is one of the smaller bush antelopes. In the arid zones of southern Africa its favorite habitat is

the transitional area between woodland vegetation and open plains. The steenbok is a highly selective feeder that eats leaves and shoots from a large variety of plants, mainly shrubs, trees and forbs. It prefers food with high nutrient concentrations like pods, berries, fruits and seeds, and grasses are eaten only during their early growth phase when nutrients accumulate at the tips of the young leaves. The steenbok may dig up roots and tubers during the dry season.

The steenbok maintains a territory throughout the year, unlike many larger antelopes that keep territories

The Damara dik-dik is the smallest antelope in southern Africa and is found in the central and northern parts of Namibia in areas with high bush cover

only during the breeding season. They remain in monogamous pairs, although, if disturbed, the male and female will flee in opposite directions. Both the male and the female deposit dung in middens that are probably markers of territory boundaries.

Springbok

The springbok is a typical resident of arid areas in southern Africa. In the past, it was known for migrating in vast numbers across areas adjoining the Kalahari Desert. Nowadays, however, because of the confinement of springbok to nature reserves and game farms, such treks no longer take place. Although it can be found in moist and arid savannas, the springbok is a plains antelope, absent from hilly and rocky habitats as well as densely vegetated areas. Furthermore, in areas where the home range overlaps with the oryx, the springbok does not venture to dunes and is confined to low-lying areas that provide better footing.

The springbok is a grazer and a browser, switching to browse when grasses are mature and dry. It also possesses the ability to drink water with much higher mineral concentrations than other species can tolerate.

However, it does not have the physiological capacities, such as the regulation of body temperature and concentration of urine, of species such as the oryx.

Like many other medium-sized antelopes, the social organization of the springbok is divided between herds of females and their young, and bachelor herds. Mixed herds are seen when males are not engaged in the maintenance of territories. Males hold small territories only for the duration of the rut, from April well into the dry season. Territorial behavior and fights between springbok males are less ritualized than among other antelopes. Nonetheless, springbok may attempt to stab in a manner similar to that of the oryx, and males may die as a result of territorial fights.

Females are not confined to the territory of one male and may wander around. Springbok breed synchronously at the beginning of the rainy season. As such, the chances of survival of individual calves are increased in the face of their predators, lions, hyenas, cheetah, wild dog and black-backed jackals. Springbok are fast runners and, in addition, will avoid chasing predators by jumping high in a peculiar leaping movement called "pronking."

Opposite:
The steenbok is a small, shy antelope common in semi-arid regions of southern Africa.

Springboks will form large herds in their favorite arid habitats in southern Africa.

Springbok busy grazing during the wet season in Etosha National Park.

Oryx

The southern African oryx, commonly called the gemsbok, is a true desert dweller which, unlike other ungulates, can subsist on little water. This species can be found in a diverse range of habitat types including stony plains and sand dunes. With its broad, high-crowned molars, the oryx can feed on coarse desert grasses that grow along drainage lines and around the base of dunes. The oryx is sensitive to small changes in the moisture content in the air and will wander over extensive distances to reach pastures that have had recent rains. Where there is no rain, however, the oryx also eats dry grass and may dig to expose roots and underground tubers.

An adult oryx drinks approximately five liters of water per day. If water is scarce, the oryx can minimize its water requirements by allowing its body temperature to rise to as high as 45°C before starting evapora-

tive cooling. Other means of minimizing water loss include concentrating urine and extracting additional moisture from feces, along with thermo-regulatory behavior such as seeking shade in the middle of the day, and feeding at night and the early hours of the morning when the moisture content of plants is higher and the temperature is cooler.

Unusually for large herbivores, oryx are found in mixed herds. Their nomadic life in the constant search for green pastures leads to inherent low population densities and infrequent encounters between herds. Associations within a herd tend to be long lasting and the relationships between individuals are associated with a stable hierarchy system headed by one bull. Although a high-ranking female normally leads while the dominant male stays at the back of a herd, the male nonetheless plays an important role in the direction and coordination of the herd's movements. Furthermore, the male will retrieve any straggler and will not hesitate to use aggression as a means of steering the herd. Although nomadic, there is evidence that some males are territorial. The territorial male may accompany a departing herd and remain in command, unless the herd enters the territory of another male. Commonly, isolated perennial water points are favorite sites for establishing territories.

With its long and spear-like horns, the oryx can cause considerable damage to an opponent. However, oryx prefer to escape large predators and are considered fast and durable runners. Aggressive behavior between oryx has been elaborated to the form of displays to mitigate the chance of injury during disputes. The hierarchical order in the herd is tested periodically, particularly if the herd is large, and also during periods of change. Most aggressive interactions are an expression of dominance by a high-ranking individual towards a low-ranking one. Male rank order is maintained with more overt aggression than female hierarchy, and includes sparring contests that may escalate to serious fights. Fights are likely to erupt when two strangers meet and compete for the same resource, be it water or an estrus female.

Zebra

A classic symbol of Africa with an enchanted call that lingers with you long after you have left the bush, the plains zebra is one of the most successful African grazers and is found in many savanna types, although its water requirements prevent the species from expanding into arid zones. It is unusual to come across a zebra in poor condition; indeed, it is generally a symbol of contentment and vigor.

Although conspicuous with its black and white coloration, the stripes are in fact an anti-predator mechanism. The large carnivores of the open savanna are color-blind – a pay-off for their superb capacity to see objects in very low-light conditions. For a lion scanning the horizon in search of prey, the stripes of the zebra will blend into the simmering heat waves. In addition, the stripes are conspicuous to other zebra seeking the security of the herd.

The southern African oryx, or gemsbok, is perhaps the antelope best adapted to survival in extreme arid conditions.

Opposite:
The Burchell's zebra found in
Etosha National Park is the
same as the plains zebra found
in East Africa.

Previous pages:
Zebra stallions fighting as
dominance hierarchies within
the herd are established.

Zebra society is based on a harem dominated by one male, the stallion. The most striking features of the harem are the absence of overt male sexual competition over mares and its permanence. Ownership over a harem is seldom disputed, if the stallion is fit, and even if the male is replaced, the composition of the harem remains intact. If a stallion shows signs of weakness, another male will try to challenge him. Old and injured stallions are replaced without being challenged. In these situations a bachelor male will start to shadow the harem and gradually take control over the harem without confronting the stallion. To establish a new harem, a stallion must first abduct a filly from her herd. He then has to fend off other males whenever she comes into heat, which occurs at monthly intervals. The competition is fierce at the initial stages of the formation of a harem, and it is unlikely that the original proprietor of a filly will be the one that remains with her after she ovulates. Additional members of the harem are acquired in a similar manner. At that stage, not only does the stallion have to keep off other males, but he also has to maintain the cohesiveness of the harem, as mares already in the harem are hostile to the newcomer. Nonetheless, within a few weeks, during which the newcomer is kept at a distance from the herd, the mares grow used to the new filly and let her in.

When not confronting stallions, males remain in bachelor herds that are led by a strong and fit adult. The ranking order in the herd is based on age, and mock fights are quite common. During a fight, the combatants rear and neck wrestle while trying to bite an ear or mane. Fights carry a serious risk of injury, particularly from kicks that reach the jaw or a leg. When a male is ready to start its own harem, it leaves the bachelor herd and wanders in search of a filly. Otherwise, the sight of a lone zebra is rare.

When hyenas approach a zebra herd, mares will hide their colts. Herds also display a good deal of cooperation to protect a sick or a weak individual. Zebra actively defend the livelihood of their fellow herd members and the stallion, in particular, does not hesitate to attack hyenas and wild dogs. Herds also show persistence in looking for missing mares or offspring following attacks by predators. Often, after a nocturnal attack by lions on a herd of zebra, the air is filled with the calls of stallions that can last long after the lions have had their share for the evening.

Zebra herds are comprised of
harems led by a stallion.

The Namib Desert

Situated on the southwestern coast of southern Africa, the Namib lies in a zone influenced by the dry air masses of subtropical anticyclones. Barren as it might seem, the Namib is relatively benign because of the cold Benguella current that moderates temperatures along the coastal desert. In addition, for perhaps one day in seven, fog bathes the Namib for some 50 kilometers inland from the coast, sustaining a complexity of plant and animal life that have adapted to utilize the moisture in the air. The resources on which this biota depends are extremely marginal. Rain rarely falls and when there is no fog, daytime temperatures soar and the heat becomes oppressive.

In the central part of the Namib, sand dunes reach the height of 300 meters. Elsewhere there are gravel plains, rocky outcrops and dry watercourses, each creating specific habitat types where different plant species grow. Many plant species are limited to particular habitats, especially along the narrow band of the Namib that lies close to the coast and in areas of higher elevation. The largest diversity of perennial vegetation occurs on the low, rocky areas where water generated from the condensation of fog supports the growth of succulent plants. Watercourses are devoid of vegetation except for the period after the rains. On gravel plains, lichens, dwarf shrubs and one endemic species that occurs nowhere else in the world, *Welwitschia mirabilis*, are the only forms of perennial plant growth.

As you move east away from the coast, however, the average rainfall increases. Here, dunes support up to ten plant species and the vegetation cover is greater. Plants tend to grow on the slopes of dunes as a result of the water-storing characteristics of the dune and the instability of the dune crests. In rocky areas, rain runoff supports the establishment of individual trees.

On approximately one day of every week, fog sweeps along the Namibian coast. The pattern of fog is a matter of life and death for many organisms that dwell in this environment.

Opposite:
Growing in central and southern parts of Namibia, the kokerboom, a member of the aloe family, is a true desert inhabitant. Early travelers observed how Bushmen used the fibrous core to make quivers for their arrows and the plant is still widely known as "the quiver tree."

Previous pages:
Granite intrusions and subsequent errosion formed the typical inselbergs in the Spitzkopje area, in the Brandberg region of Namibia.

"Dune 45" is a popular site in the Sossesvlei canyon that leads deep into the sand dunes of the Namib Desert.

Sand sifts through the relics of Kolmanskop – a mining town situated ten kilometers east of Lüderitz. The town flourished earlier this century, but was abandoned after mining operations ceased in 1950.

In the absence of fire and termites, dead tree trunks last many years in the dry desert climate.

Right:
The old port of Lüderitz on the shores of the Atlantic Ocean has a unique old colonial German atmosphere blended into its African surroundings.

Opposite:
The base of dunes shelters its own habitat that enables plants to grow that may in turn serve as food source to this lone oryx.

The stony desolation of the Namib Naukluft Park is interrupted by the growth of plants that have adapted to survival in such dry conditions, like this cactus that stores water in its stems.

Right:
Spring in the desert is rich with florescence.

The plains, on the other hand, are largely bare except after the rains when there is some grass cover for a short period. On the 100mm-isohyet, fog rarely occurs, yet because of their increased storage of rainwater, dunes support a higher cover of grass species and the establishment of plants is more vigorous. Acacia trees and perennial shrubs become common on the dry watercourses, while the rocky hills support quite a number of tree, shrubs and large succulent species. However, it is only further inland where the rainfall averages over 150mm a year, that perennial vegetation is more established and creates a continuous cover across the landscape.

Plants in the desert

Many animal species are able to withstand the harsh conditions of the desert by avoiding extreme conditions and moving to more favorable areas. Plants, however, have to display far greater tolerance, as they cannot escape so easily from the extremes of the desert environment. Deep root development and the growth of small leaves or large succulent stems without leaves are the most prominent forms of morphological adaptations among plants to arid conditions. The orientation of leaves is also an important function as it determines the exposure of surface area to light for photosynthesis as well as exposure to heat radiation. For example, vertically oriented surfaces such as the stems of cacti absorb less solar energy and remain cooler than leaves that are oriented at right angles to the rays of the sun. In addition, plants with an east-west orientation gain more heat than those oriented south-north. Since the vegetation cover in the desert is extremely sparse, plants cannot rely on the proximity of other vegetation for shade or to create favorable microclimates for growth.

Among cacti and other plants, spines not only deter herbivores, but also reduce heat loads by increasing reflectance and creating an isolating layer of air between the spines and the surface of the plant. However, heat loss in such plants is slower at night by comparison to plants without a dense spine cover. Some plants have gone to the extreme where the plant grows beneath the soil surface with only the leaf tips appear-ing above the surface. Even more impressive is a species of cactus that lives entirely under the surface with only its flowers protruding.

The nature of the plant cuticle plays an important role in the determination of the rate of water loss. Most water loss in plants is a result of transpiration through the open stomata. The thickness of the cuticular wax layer and the concentration of lipid depositions determine the rate of water loss from the surface of the plant. Hence, plants that are well adapted to the conditions of the desert close their stomata during the hottest time of the day to minimize water loss.

Tenebrionid beetles

Tenebrionid beetles, common residents of the Namib Desert, have been a popular research topic because of their remarkable adaptation to the specific conditions found there. For example, the black color of many animal species in the desert seems puzzling because it has a higher heat absorption rate, but in fact the black melanin compound that provides the protective cover of the tenebrionid beetle has waterproofing properties that override the disadvantage of color.

A tenebrionid beetle struggles up a dune.

The densities of beetles of the kind that feed on detritus are fairly low in deserts where not much vegetation cover exists, mostly because the lack of moisture poses a significant limitation for fungal and microbial decomposers. Hence, the function of the tenebrionid beetle is vital for the maintenance of nutrient cycling. Wind-blown plant and other material accumulate at the base of the dunes and provide a food source for the beetles. However, for the purpose of digesting this food, beetles require water, so they utilize the regular occurrence of fog along the dune belt close to the shore by emerging at night when fog occurs and climbing to the crest of a dune where fog condensation is the greatest. Close to the crest, the beetles adopt a head-down stance facing into the fog-bearing wind. Fog droplets condense on the wing covers of the beetles, the elytra, and trickle down to their mouth parts. The rate of water gain can reach as much as 34 percent of body water content.

Another beetle species, *Lepidochora Sp.*, employs a much more sophisticated system. These nocturnal beetles construct narrow trenches on the surface of the sand perpendicular to the direction of the wind. The ridges of the trenches collect much more water than the surrounding sand. When they return to the trench, the beetles flatten the ridges and extract water from the sand to drink.

Desert lizards

Of all vertebrate classes, reptiles have adapted best to the harsh and extreme arid conditions of the desert. Lizards and other reptiles escape hostile conditions during heat stress through brumation, the term for reptilian aestivation. Like hibernation, aestivation rep-

A gecko can climb on smooth and vertical surfaces using soft lamellas at the tips of its digits.

resents a condition of prolonged dormancy or torpor during which the metabolic rate and body temperature are significantly reduced. Animals that do not regulate their internal body temperature usually have to seek a cool and moist microhabitat and their metabolic rate is markedly reduced. The duration of brumation depends on the reserves of fat that reptiles accumulate prior to entering the brumation phase. Water loss is very much reduced in desert-adapted reptiles by molecules containing lipids that are imbedded in the skin and integument of lizards, and prevent the loss of water. In addition, reptiles produce highly concentrated urine.

The ability to reproduce successfully is also a significant obstacle in the adaptation of animals to arid conditions. Desert reptiles have adopted a range of reproductive strategies. Some lizards have a short lifespan with relatively high reproductive output. Others have become adapted to a slower reproductive rate and long lifespan. Climate and habitat types are equally influential on reproduction: for example, in areas such as the fog belt of the Namib dunes, the climate is relatively stable, resulting in the reproduction of lizards throughout the year. All reptiles develop in eggs, although some reptile species maintain the eggs in their body and brood them until the birth of young. If conditions are extreme, reptiles will seek out a suitable place with a stable microclimate where they will lay their eggs. Conversely, if conditions are relatively stable, the reptiles are able to maintain the eggs in their body and thus withstand exposure. This strategy provides a physical protection to the eggs that is otherwise lacking when the eggs are left in a nest within reach of predators.

The agama is a common lizard in arid environments.

Using its webbed feet as air brakes, a pelican makes a final approach for landing.

Opposite:
Cape Gannets are common offshore sea birds that accompany the migration of sardines eastward along the coast to KwaZulu-Natal in South Africa.

Right:
Cape cormorants breed in colonies on islands off the West Coast of Namibia. Their nest is made up from sticks and seaweed.

Sea birds

Cape gannets form colonies on rocky islands and other isolated spots along the Namib coast. Large numbers of these birds accompany schools of pilchards and mackerel up the West Coast of Namibia and the East Coast of South Africa. When feeding, they regularly dive from considerable heights into the sea.

Cape cormorants share some of their distribution range and breeding grounds with the Cape gannets. These marine birds are migratory, flying in long lines low above the surface of the sea in a rippling wave-like manner.

Pelican

The unmistakable pelican is white with black flight feathers; the white feathers turn pinkish during the breeding season. Pelicans are well adapted to fishing for large quantities of small fish. The pattern of fishing is well coordinated among the members of the flock: they form a line and drive the fish into shallow water, where they are scooped up and collected in the pelican's large pouch. Pelicans frequent bays and river mouths along the West Coast of Namibia where shallow water is found.

59

In a flurry of excitement, flamingos erect their body feathers.

Left:
In the cool hours of the early mornings, flamingos retain their heads under their wings to keep themselves warm.

The greater flamingo flocks to the shallow lagoons of the West Coast of Namibia. They feed on tiny crustaceans that thrive in the saline water.

Flamingo

With extremely long legs and necks, flamingos are able to wade in fairly deep water in their search for food. To feed, the flamingo inserts its bill in the water in an inverted position. The upper bill, which is smaller than the lower one, is bent and has rows of dents like a comb. This specialized structure is a modification for filtering small animal matter in the mud. While feeding, the flamingo wades through muddy water, zigzagging its head from side to side. Through back-and-forth movements of its large, fleshy tongue and by straining the water out through its bill, the flamingo collects chironomid larvae, other insect larvae, shrimps and small mollusks.

The flamingo's toes are webbed which allows it to swim in deeper water. It is a highly gregarious bird, and with its scarlet plumage beautiful to watch. Its diet determines the hues of scarlet in the plumage – if there is a greater concentration of microscopic algae that harbor red pigments in the water, the flamingo tends to be more reddish. Although the flamingo is commonly associated with aquatic environments, in southern Africa it can be found in desolate areas miles from the nearest large body of water. Flamingos gather in large pans, such as Etosha in Namibia and the Makgadikgadi in northern Botswana, following good rainfall that has formed large shallow sheets of water. However, they are reliably found only in suitable shallow coastal lagoons, as their nests are made in large colonies in muddy flats. These are formed from mounds of mud with a hollow depression at the top for the clutch of two eggs.

Cape fur seal

Among the most impressive sights (if you can ignore the accompanying smell) along parts of the Namibian coast are the breeding colonies of Cape fur seal. Breeding sites are located predominantly on rocky shores, although flat, sandy beaches are also suitable. Males haul out and establish their territories onshore about mid-October. Females follow a few weeks later and drop a single pup each. The pups suckle within an hour after birth and the females come into estrus within a week of the birth of the pup. Mating occurs while the female attends her pup. The female ventures out to sea to feed and locates her pup by the sound of bleating or by using scent.

The maternal bond between the female and her pup is strong during the first few days after birth, but the pup itself is even more responsible for the maintenance of a strong bond. As they grow, young pups congregate on playgrounds. Gradually, they explore the vicinity, if ponds and places of quiet water exist. By the end of the third month after birth, the mother may be absent from her pup for long periods. In turn, the pups explore deeper water and acquire proficiency in swimming. Juvenile seals form discrete peer groups on the beach. A female attains sexual maturity by the age of three, when she will leave her group and follow the pattern of the adults, hauling out to join the males and females on the breeding grounds.

When males first arrive on the breeding grounds, their blubber is already loaded with fat. Those that establish a territory do not move off it for more than a month. The maintenance of territory boundaries and

herding females mean the males expend considerable amounts of energy. Males arriving later at the breeding sites have considerable difficulty in establishing their territories. In crowded conditions, males will vigorously defend their territory. Fights are frequent and involve chest to chest confrontations, each protagonist trying to throw his opponent off balance. Serious wounds are not infrequent. Fights can escalate if the contestants move into the territory of a third male, which will then attack and bite indiscriminately. Although the crowded conditions can give an alternative impression, females remain within a chosen male's territory to escape harm and shelter their pups. Females also seek space within the male's territory, which can result in serious fights between females that are sometimes settled by the male.

The population of the Cape fur seal on the Namibian coast is one of two large concentrations of the species that occur in the southern oceans, the other being confined to the coasts and islands of Australia and Tasmania. The seals range more than 100 kilometers out in to the open seas and forage independently, but small groups may feed together if food sources are clustered. Most of the food taken by the Cape fur seal is from schools of small fish, including pilchards and Cape mackerel. Rock lobsters and other crustaceans as well as squids are also eaten, but to a lesser extent. Fur seals tend to congregate in the vicinity of trawlers and around 4000 die annually as a result of becoming entangled in nets, although this number is small in relation to the total size of the seal population. The seal population on the west coast of southern Africa is also subject to annual culling, the reason being that excessive numbers of seals damage commercial fishing through reducing fish quantities and damage to nets. Conversely, seals may be affected by the reduction of fish populations due to improved techniques for locating and capturing fish. In any case, over-exploitation of fish stocks by commercial fishing companies increases the competition with seals for a mutual resource, which triggers further conflict between seals and people.

Left:
A breeding colony of Cape fur seals mass along a remote beach on the Skeleton Coast. The seal has a characteristic sexual dimorphism with males much larger than females.

Bubbling with Life –
Bushveld of Lapalala and Sabi-Sand

I dearly wanted to stay in the Namibian Desert to continue following the mysterious ways of animal behavior. However, my plans did not work out and knowing that African wildlife carries its allure wherever animals wander freely, I decided not to wait. Practicalities also mattered. I was running out of money and research funds were scarce. Under the auspices of Pretoria University, I had to settle for something more modest and that did not pose the formidable logistical obstacles of remote places.

Although it is completely unlike Etosha, Lapalala Wilderness has its own appeal. Hidden in the cradle of the Waterberg highlands of northern South Africa, the reserve is far from the crowds although it is only three hours' drive from Johannesburg. At the time I came to do my research there, the concept of private game reserves in areas outside the Eastern Transvaal was in its infancy. Only those who could afford to buy land and support the infrastructure were

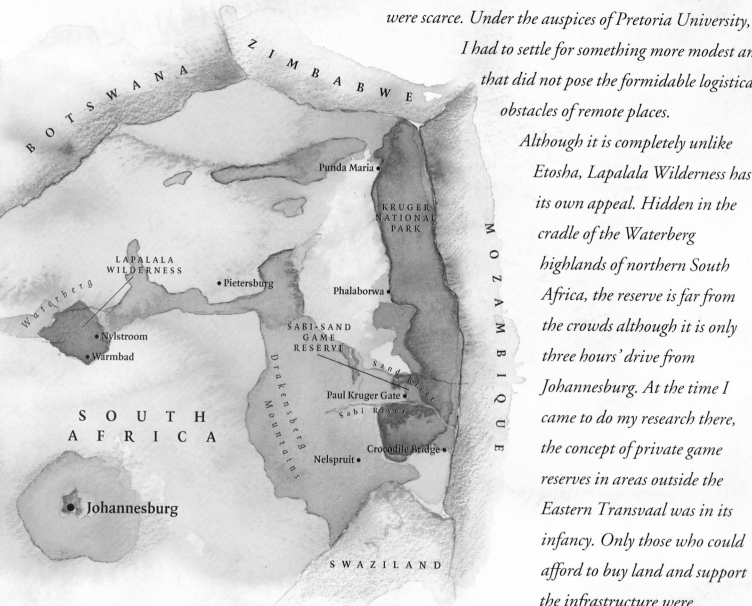

privileged enough to have their properties declared nature reserves. The common belief was that without the "Big Five" – namely lion, rhino, elephant, buffalo and leopard – tourists would not come. Lapalala Wilderness was among the first private game reserves in South Africa to display its faith in its indigenous wildlife and attempt to introduce species that had become locally extinct as a result of human activity. This was good enough for me. I longed for the animals of Africa, wherever they were in the wild and the conservation issue added meaning to my stay in the bush.

Although the opportunity to share the world of animals was much more limited in the dense bush and rugged terrain of the Waterberg, I nevertheless thrived in the company of the small creatures that lived around the cabin where I stayed alone in the bush. When I was much younger, somebody had told me that you learn about your space through walking. My experience in Lapalala revealed a lot of the truth in that remark. My approach to photography also changed, as I would plan ahead and anticipate the shots I would take and the angles of light I would encounter during long walks. It was another reminder that there are many more aspects to the bush than simply large animals.

When it came, the transfer of my research from the Waterberg to the lowveld of the Eastern Transvaal was not as dramatic as that from Etosha to Lapalala. My motivation for moving a few hundred kilometers eastwards was to find a more lucrative research topic for my doctorate. In Sabi-Sand, I had an opportunity to examine in-depth the relationships between the soil, vegetation and large herbivores in a game reserve that was bubbling with life. The bush was still dense, but the animals were tamer and allowed some intrusion into their private lives. Occasional glimpses of game soon became a flood of colors, reflections and stories as I grew to know the animals of the Sabi-Sabi Sand.

Lapalala Wilderness

Lapalala Wilderness is a private game reserve situated in the northeastern part of the Waterberg region of the Northern Province in South Africa. The region is an elevated highland area between 1000 and 3500 meters above sea level, the main escarpment forming a rugged and densely vegetated territory that falls away gradually to the west and overlooks the Upper Limpopo Valley. The compacted brown and red rocks found here are mainly of volcanic origin. Sandstone is also common and occurs in thick beds that are either pebbly or gritty.

Within the undulating hills that comprise the Waterberg Plateau, several perennial rivers arise. Of these, the Palala, with its steep canyons and narrow ravines, is the major rivercourse traversing the reserve. The vegetation in Lapalala is classified as sour bush-veld, a type that covers extensive areas of the central and northern parts of southern Africa. Sour bushveld (or sourveld) means that the nutritive value of grass deteriorates rapidly during the dry winter. The vegetation is comprised of deciduous plants without spines and open drainage-line grasslands at the bottom of hills. The productivity of herbaceous plants is usually high and tends to be dominated by tall perennial species.

Since its early settlement the Waterberg region has always been sparsely inhabited. The first human imprint was by hunter-gatherers on the rocks of the area, but the scarcity of low-lying land with highly enriched soils meant that the land was useless for intensive agriculture, forcing people to leave for areas with more fertile grounds. In addition, the acidid soils which gave rise to thick vegetation and low nutrient contents in grasses inhibited the maintaining of herds of livestock, and, as a result, much of the farmland in the region was lightly stocked and underdeveloped. On the other hand, such conditions enabled wildlife to find refuge in the less accessible parts of the area, including Lapalala where, for example, a core population of indigenous roan antelope survived.

Pages 64–65:
The Waterberg Plateau in the northern part of South Africa is situated on granitoid rocks that give rise to acidic soils. The combination of high rainfall with these soils gives rise to unique vegetation forms.

Opposite:
Rivers and streams cleave the Waterberg Plateau and add much diversity to this otherwise rugged and densely vegetated terrain.

In contrast to its habits in East Africa, wildebeest in southern Africa tend to form small herds and aggregations. This pair of bulls was fleeing from a helicopter which was conducting an aerial survey in the Lapalala Wilderness.

Bushmen paintings indicate that the Waterberg was home to South Africa's earliest inhabitants.

Left:
The leaves of the Kudu berry become distinctly colored as the dry winter sets in around the Waterberg.

Opposite:
For all the diversity of plant species in the Waterberg region, large herbivores are not abundant and one has to keep a vigilant eye in the bush to spot a shy kudu or duiker.

Blow flies cluster on the exposed intestines of a giraffe.

Opposite:
The robber fly predates on other insects that it catches in the air. The powerful mouth parts can pierce the tough carapace of small beetles.

Page 72:
Lichens represent a form of plant growth that features traits of both fungi and algae.

Page 73:
A praying mantis camouflages itself to hide from its enemies and to obtain prey.

Flies

Over 85,000 species of flies have been described and there seem to be almost as many species still to be described. Fly species belong to the order Diptera, and are distinguished from other insects in that they have only one pair of membranous wings. Although there are insects other than flies that have one pair of wings, none of these insects share with flies their special structure and adaptations, such as the hind wings that are reduced to tiny knobbed structures that function as a balance during flight.

The morphology of the adult fly is quite complex. The head consists of the eyes, antennae and mouth parts. The eye usually occupies most of the side of the head, except in some parasite flies where the eyes have, in fact, become redundant. The mouth parts form a tubular organ called the proboscis. Two types of proboscis can be distinguished, namely the piercing, such as that found on the mosquito, xand the sucking, as is found on the housefly.

Robber flies represent a distinct family that range in size from 3mm to 40mm. In some tropical areas they may even reach a size of up to 7.5 cm – specimens this large manage to overpower bees and wasps quite easily. Three rudimentary eyes are located between the compound eyes and probably assist in the perception of light and shadow. Their perception of movement is highly advanced in contrast to their ability to discern details. Robber flies, therefore, tend to hunt anything that moves. Its larvae live in the soil or burrow into wood. The adults are exclusively carnivorous, feeding on living prey, usually caught in flight. The proboscis is well developed for this purpose, and is able to pierce the strong carapace of small dung beetles.

Big-headed flies have very large hemispherical heads, consisting almost entirely of eye. These flies have a slow, delicate, hovering flight between grasses and low vegetation. The larvae parasite the insides of bees and cicadas. When fully developed, the larva occupies most of the host's abdomen.

A young Nile monitor on the defense. Adult monitors will normally scramble for the safety of nearby water.

Previous pages:
The tongue of the white throated monitor can detect minute concentrations of scent carried in the air. Like most other reptiles, its sense of smell is a vital component in its orientation.

Nile monitor

These large lizards are quite common throughout sub-Saharan Africa. A semi-aquatic reptile with a flat, elongated tail that it uses to propel itself in water, it eats crocodile eggs and a variety of creatures found around water, such as crabs and mussels, as well as small mammals and birds. During the day, monitors are never far from water and are often found basking in the sun in open spaces or on rocks and branches of trees. The Nile monitor takes refuge in water and can swim considerable distances under water, if pursued. Their main defensive weapon is their tail, which can inflict severe and well-directed blows. They also may sham dead for hours until danger has passed.

In the lowveld, during the early summer, Nile monitors hunt around rapids where migrating shoals of fish are caught in large numbers as they scramble among the rocks on their way up-stream to their breeding grounds. The eggs of the Nile monitor are laid in a hole dug by the female deep in a termite mound or a sand bank. The young emerge in early spring and make off instinctively to the safe haven of the nearest water.

White throated monitor

Typical savanna dwellers, these terrestrial lizards are expert climbers of rocks and trees. Unlike the water-dependent Nile monitor, the leguaan, as the white throated monitor is called in South Africa, seldom remains in one locality for any length of time. Normally they are found in rock crevices, but may occupy holes in the ground and trees. In comparison to the Nile monitor, the leguaan appears more sluggish as it forages for its food. However, if confronted, the leguaan adopts a menacing pose, inflating its throat and hissing loudly. It will lash out with its tail and bite fiercely at any object within reach. In Lapalala Wilderness, I had many encounters with the leguaan. Those that did not escape held firmly to nearby objects. Studying them closely, I was amazed to see the large number of ticks on their body, especially in places such as the ear openings that are beyond the reach of its long tongue.

The leguaan is able to abstain from drinking water and survive on the fluids it obtains from its prey. Their diet mainly consists of small mammals, birds and their eggs, other reptiles and insects. Leguaans swallow their prey entirely and the digestion process may take a long time. Eagles and other raptors are their main enemies, although upon being caught, the leguaan will fight back voraciously and may sometimes gain the upper hand in a struggle.

An ostrich encounter

During the breeding season, ostrich males become territorial and will utter a dull roar which, at a distance, can sound very much like the roar of a lion. In Lapalala Wilderness, several ostriches were kept more as the inheritance of the new owners than strictly for the purposes of wildlife rehabilitation.

One day, as I set off to count roan antelope, I spotted a male ostrich at the edge of a clearing. It was handsome, with large red scales on the sheen of each leg. This was a good photographic opportunity, as the male was approaching with determined strides, exposing his legs to the early morning light. I took a photograph, put the camera away in my small backpack, and headed off. Then I heard the dash of feet behind me. The male had decided to chase me away and foolishly I started running, forgetting how fast ostriches can run. Within seconds, the ostrich caught up and gave me two strong kicks in the behind. My shirt and part of my jeans were torn, and I was furious. As this was at an early stage in my bush experience, I had practically had no previous encounters with hostile wildlife. It seemed rather absurd to be attacked by a bird. (Never mind that it was more than twice my weight.) In a rage, I turned around to face the ostrich. Not stopping to think about the situation I was in, I grabbed its neck and with both hands brought its head to my level. I slapped it across the face twice, then squeezed its neck to make my point clear. Without knowing it, I had managed to disarm the ostrich, as by bringing its head down, I had prevented the ostrich from kicking and pushing against me. However, the ostrich kept roaring in spite of my tight grip, so I looked around in desperation. There was a clump of bushes and trees not far away. Surely, I thought, I could drag the ostrich to the bushes and release it and then reach the safety of the bush without much effort.

An African image – ostriches at sunset.

During the course of my field-work in Lapalala Wilderness, Andreas would follow me carrying a yardstick to measure the degree of vegetation cover.

So I tried to drag the ostrich, but its hundred-plus kilograms were rooted to the ground. Despair began to creep over me, but gradually I felt the ostrich showing signs of weakness. I waited a bit, still holding the bird's neck, but then decided it was safe to let it go. The ostrich swayed and I ran for cover, which I managed to get to before it could recover his senses.

I later learned that a kick from an ostrich can inflict serious injuries, if not kill you. The robust, sharp talon at the tip of its foot can easily slash through the skin and reach internal organs. As it turned out, the attack that I sustained was the first of several attempts on the reserve's staff. The pugnacious ostrich was caught and relocated to a distant part of the reserve isolated from visitors.

Genet

The genet is found wherever there is sufficient cover for it to hide and food to eat. It feeds on small vertebrates such as rodents, bats, birds, lizards, snakes and frogs, as well as insects and fruits. It tends to forage after dark, stalking and ambushing its prey.

Genets operate primarily through the olfactory sense, and it appears that they can distinguish different scents and discriminate between individuals. They will mark prominent objects in their territory, secreting the fluid through their anal glands. Scent marking is intensified in males during the mating season when they seek females.

Females raise their young in a hole or a nest of leaves, killing prey for them until the kittens are mature enough to learn the secrets of foraging and hunting. In their nocturnal habits, genets are shy and elusive creatures, and their presence is often evident only through the spoor they leave on tracks. Although the genet is relatively common throughout southern Africa, Lapalala Wilderness was the only area where I was able to see them almost every night. It may be that in the large game reserves, where there are large carnivores, genets tend to be more elusive. Leopards, for example, will readily take them. In Lapalala, genets frequented my house as well as other camp sites searching for scraps of food.

Roan

Once widely distributed in woodland savannas of Africa, the roan suffered from extensive poaching and habitat destruction. Roan densities were never high anywhere and it is now considered a threatened species in South Africa. Although large in size, the roan is a selective grazer on perennial grasses that grow on well-drained soils with a poor nutrient content. As

such, the roan is unique in utilizing habitats that otherwise support a relatively low herbivore biomass. During the dry season, the roan will revert to some browsing on forbs and leaves, but it is relatively dependent on water and will stay in the vicinity of watersources during the dry season.

Roan maintain a sedentary and territorial social structure, remaining in small herds throughout southern Africa. A herd consists of females and young that share a traditional and exclusive home range. The composition of herds varies and it seems that social

Genets were nocturnal visitors in campsites at Lapalala. The asymmetry in the eyes shows that this genet – which had become my house guest was blind in its right eye.

Roan bull courting a female.

bonds within the immature classes are stronger than between mothers and young. Males are tolerated in the female herd until they reach adolescence at about two years of age. After leaving the natal herd, young males join bachelor herds where they remain until maturity in their sixth year. At normal population densities, the home range of a female herd overlaps with several male territories. The territorial males patrol their boundaries frequently and deposit dung at intervals. Roan may also thrash and rub small trees and shrubs to demarcate boundaries.

Cows give birth away from the herd. The more dominant the cow, the shorter the isolation period between giving birth and re-joining the herd, but the period does not normally last more than a week.

Mother and calf communicate through calls as it is often difficult to maintain eye contact in the thick bush. Although a relatively slow animal, the predation level on roan is low, if the calf survives its first few months. A combination of factors, such as light roan densities, light predator densities, alertness and their large size contribute to the small influence of large predators on roan populations.

Roan conservation was the main topic in my master's thesis. Under the auspices of the Mammal Research Institute of Pretoria University, I set out to assess the potential for establishing roan populations in their former range in the Waterberg. Traditionally, roan herds were abundant in the region before the encroachment of settlements and agriculture that eliminated favorable habitats. However, the poor nutritional value of natural fodder and the low potential of the Waterberg plateau for agriculture meant that the area remained largely undeveloped and provided a refuge for roan. In the early 1960s, the Provincial Department of Conservation captured several roans and transferred the animals to nature reserves on the fringes of the Waterberg region.

Roan bred successfully in their new home and it was decided that surplus animals could be rehabilitated to their former range. In an unprecedented move, the Provincial Administration approved the translocation of several roans to a private nature reserve, Lapalala Wilderness. I was to monitor the progress of the roan following their release in Lapalala. The new arrivals joined existing herds of roan, and in the section of the reserve I monitored, there were approximately twelve roan distributed throughout a 2000-hectare block.

My fieldwork mainly consisted of locating roan and other large herbivores and carefully noting their location and activities. Ultimately, I wanted to be able to assess the habitat preferences of the animals with respect to the availability of all the resources. Factors such as topography, rockiness, soil nutrients, grass cover and composition, abundance of shrub and tree species and the degree of visibility through the vegetation were all analyzed.

Sightings of roan were sporadic and I never saw more than three individuals in a herd. The roan concentrated on the northern part of the reserve, an elevated plateau with sparse woodland savanna vegetation that was typical roan habitat. My final analysis however, indicated that, although there was some preference to this type of vegetation, the roan did not show any affinity to a particular factor. This led me to believe that conditions in the area were marginal for roan and that the survival chances were fair but not optimal.

Interestingly, I also followed a large group of sable that had also been introduced to the reserve. According to the text books, sable preferred denser woodland savannas than the roan, but my research indicated that sable had no real preference and that their location through the study area was more or less random. I concluded that the chances of survival of sable were better and that management efforts should prioritize breeding of sable. However, I was proved wrong.

Within five years of the submission of my thesis, most of the sable had died while the roan maintained their numbers. The lesson proved again that theories based on scientific evidence might not eventually happen. Nevertheless, there was some value in conducting research that will back up conservation and management practices. Although some of the conclusions were incorrect, this study provided the managers of

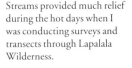

Streams provided much relief during the hot days when I was conducting surveys and transects through Lapalala Wilderness.

the reserve with invaluable information about the ecology of the area and some of the natural processes that take place.

White rhinoceros

The white or square-lipped rhinoceros is the largest of the grazers. Its wide, square mouth enables it to mow dense swards of short grass, in contrast to the black rhinoceros that has a pointed lip for browsing the leaves of trees and shrubs. The origin of the name is probably a misinterpretation of the Afrikaans name for the animal, "wyd" or wide, lip, which became "white" to English-speaking settlers.

Female white rhino have overlapping home ranges, and tend to associate with sub-adults, mostly their recent offspring. They are rarely solitary, and juveniles may attach themselves transiently to another cow with a calf. Stable herds up to six individuals may be formed if calfless cows join and allow foreign juveniles into their group.

Unlike cows and adolescents, adult bulls are mostly solitary. Males hold territories for a tenure of about three years. For every territory there are two or three satellite males. The owner of the territory is conditioned to the presence of particular individual males and ignores them as long as they do not challenge his dominance whenever they encounter each other.

Unlike the temperamental black rhino, the white rhino is seldom aggressive except for territorial disputes between males. When territorial bulls meet at the border of adjoining territorial areas, both assert dominance. One may fake a charge by trotting up with lowered head, checking at the last moment. Typically, however, both males will walk up with their heads raised and stand horn to horn staring at each other. If the intruder does not display submission by dropping his head and putting his ears back, a fight may ensue. The two will back off and rub their horns against the ground, although they sometimes clash horns. Attempts to take over a territory or to head off

Opposite:
The coarse appearance of the rhino skin gives no indication of its sensitivity.

No matter how big they are, white rhinos blend well into the background of the bush.

Translocating a rhino is not a simple matter. The rhino is partially sedated so that it can be manipulated on to the back of the truck.

an estrus cow that is about to enter a neighboring territory may result in a fight. Females and adolescent males, on the other hand, are seldom confronted.

White rhino use a diverse range of vocalization to communicate. When confronting a territorial male, the intruder might back away trumpeting to diffuse the tension. Similarly, an adult male that has no intention of confronting the territorial bull may scream for mercy while rebuffing an attack. Mother and infant interactions involve a repertoire of sounds that vary from whining when the calf begs, to squeaking when the calf is in distress. While courting, the male may try to prevent the departure of the female from his territory by emitting a loud wailing sound.

Olfactory communication is important in the demarcation of territories. A territorial male maintains some 20 to 30 dung middens that serve as permanent scent stations. When it drops dung, the male scatters and excavates the pile by kicking it. The older the midden site, the larger the diameter of dung deposits. Dung beetles make extensive use of the dung, forming balls to provide food for their young. Francolins, guinea fowl and other birds, as well as reptiles and mongoose, will also frequent the site in search of edible and undigested plant parts.

Although mild by nature, the white rhino will not hesitate to charge if it feels threatened. This is particularly true in the case of a mother defending her offspring. During the early days of my stay in the bush, when its ways were not yet obvious to me, I was taught

a lesson by a white rhino. Lapalala Wilderness had received a group of ten female and male rhino that were quick to establish themselves in the rugged terrain of the Waterberg. A small group that included a female, a territorial bull and three juveniles settled not far from the entrance to the reserve. It seems that couch grass, a short and nutritious type of grass, and a dam were the major attractions for the rhinos. One afternoon, on my way back to my cabin, I noticed the family lying peacefully underneath the shade of a tree in the middle of an open area. At that time I did not have any decent photographs of rhino, so I ran up the hill to my cabin, picked up my camera and tripod, and came back to find the rhinos. I moved slowly in the open field, getting into a position where I could set my tripod and take the photographs. I was close enough to see the small clouds of dust rising from the ground as they exhaled air through their nostrils.

I took several photos and was about to leave when the bush suddenly exploded into life. The rhinos had noticed that I was there and were on their feet before I could collect my equipment. As the dust settled, I saw to my horror that there was a small calf standing among the adults. Without waiting to see how they responded, I started running towards the safety of the thick bush, hoping to find a tall tree to climb. Unfortunately, the bush was a bit far. I heard the heavy foot steps of the rhino behind me, and I looked back to see three rhinos, headed by the calf, running after me. I could hear the heavy puffing of air coming from their nostrils and feel the earth trembling. I braced myself for impact but then began to realize that I should have been overtaken by now. I stopped, and watched the rhinos heading into the bush a few meters away from me. The reason for this is that white rhino calves will head for their retreat route while the mother covers behind. This is unlike black rhinos, where the reverse occurs. Although the calf was heading in my direction, it decided to change its course at the last moment, undoubtedly saving me. Two years later, another student studying rhinos in Natal was charged under similar circumstances. Unfortunately this time, the calf did not change direction and the student was killed by the mother.

The southern African white rhino is a conservation success story. During the early 1800s, greed and hunting brought a dramatic decline in the numbers of rhino. Fortunately, the foresight of few people allowed the establishment of game reserves in Natal, South Africa in the late 1800s, to save the species from extinction. The results were astonishing. Within a short period, the population of the white rhino proliferated. Being roughage eaters, rhinos are not highly selective grazers and will eat various kinds of grass species as long as there is also an ample supply of water. The rhino population grew to the extent that it was decided that since rhino densities in the Natal reserve were high, it would be beneficial to propagate rhinos to remote reserves situated within their former distribution range. Thus white rhinos were translocated from Umfolozi to other reserves such as Mkuzi and the Kruger National Park. Nowadays, the translocation of rhinos is a common occurrence. Due to the fact that the National Parks in South Africa are fully stocked with white rhinos (provided that the park has suitable habitats), private game reserves also receive surplus animals.

Similar attempts were made for the conservation of the black rhinoceros. While on the brink of extinction throughout Africa, black rhinos are abundant in protected reserves in Natal. As part of the conservation effort, black rhinos are translocated to game reserves that provide a true natural sanctuary and adequate protection for the newcomers. Lapalala Wilderness was one of the first private game reserves in South Africa to accept black rhinos.

The translocation of rhinos between nature reserves involves considerable logistics and special techniques to ensure the safety and welfare of the animal. Just catching a rhino requires a coordinated group effort. A rhino can run over rugged terrain at 40 kilometers per hour, and thus the most common method to capture rhinos is by helicopter. They are shot with a dart loaded with a special anesthetic, which has colourful feathers to indicate the location of the dart on the back or side of the animal. The helicopter then follows the rhino to the place where it settles down and calls for the ground team. This is the easy part. The ground team arrives with a heavy truck and trailer. After verifying the physical condition of the rhino, a small dose of anti-anesthetic is injected into a vein in the ear. With the help of the winch and a group of strong men, the rhino is loaded into the trailer. A competent group can capture and load a rhino onto the truck within a couple of hours. Depending on the distance and the conditions at the destination, the rhino may receive additional treatment before it is released in its new home.

Thanks to the vision and efforts of Clive Walker and his wife Conita, Lapalala Wilderness was established on the grounds of an old cattle farm. Later on it became a breeding center for the black rhino in South Africa.

The Sabi-Sand

Located in the northeastern part of South Africa, the Lowveld lies underneath the Great Escarpment of the eastern Transvaal region. A stretch of land west of the well-known Kruger National Park that comprises various private game reserves of which the Sabi-Sand consortium is one of the most prominent. This region is composed of moderately dissected, gently rounded hill country that rises between 100 and 200 meters above the floor of the Sand River valley. Most of the area is on ancient granite bedrock cut through by intrusions of younger volcanic rocks, forming a grid of dikes, or narrow lines of solid rock that add much to the variety of habitat types. As the rocks have disintegrated over millions of years, a fine black cotton soil has formed, which is rich in minerals that nourish a variety of plant species. The mean annual rainfall classifies the majority of the region as a semi-arid savanna ecosystem. Many rivers cross the Lowveld flowing from west to east. The Sabi-Sand area, located between Gazankulu settlements in the west and the Kruger National Park in the east, is naturally encased by the Sabie and the Sand rivers. The Sand River forms the main perennial water base line which runs obliquely across the center of the reserve. Drainage and catchment basins funnel in to this river and the Sabie River in the south.

Opposite:
The Lowveld region supports a diverse fauna and flora. With an annual rainfall of about 500mm it is classified as a semi-arid savanna.

The early hours of the morning are, perhaps, the best time in the bush. Between the vapor of mist, impala are beginning to forage for suitable vegetation.

Soils develop in distinctive caternary sequences on the granitoid rocks. In other words, during a period measured on a geological scale, soil is formed from the parent rock material and is washed down the catena – a gentle hill – to the valley, during an erosion process.

At the foot of the slope, the fine particles of soil are deposited and form impermeable clay horizons. The vegetation in the area is greatly influenced by both rainfall patterns and soil properties. The landscape is characterized by bushveld or savanna vegetation, which, owing to the absence of climatic and topographic barriers in the north, has a close resemblance to that of tropical African savanna. Bushveld includes low woody vegetation that branches close to the ground, an effect enhanced by regular fires. In some areas the bushveld gives way to mature woodlands that form dense stands of trees with long straight trunks.

One of the most intriguing aspects of the dynamics of plant communities in savanna ecosystems is the balance between trees and grasses. Typically, savanna areas are characterized by their prolific diversity and abundance of grass species. Interspersed between grass pastures, shrub and tree species may also develop. It seems that the water-holding capacity of soil is responsible for the maintenance of any given balance between grasses and trees. At times, however, this delicate equilibrium may be interrupted as a result of a fast water depletion from the upper soil layers. As a result, the vigorous grass growth gives way to the encroachment of woody plants. During the course of my research in the Sabi-Sand, I found that rainfall patterns had much to do with encroachment. It seems

The nutritious value of grass is at its peak during the height of the wet season before seeding takes place, when nutrients are pumped from the roots to promote leaf and shoot growth. Herbivores that eat during the early hours of the morning benefit from the high moisture content of the grasses.

Pages 88–89:
Rainfall is the pivotal factor behind the annual events of plant growth and animal reproduction. Rainfall mainly occurs in sporadic thunderstorms between spells of sunshine.

The term woodland savanna was coined to describe areas that support grasslands intersected by shrubs and trees.

Savanna grasslands have a plethora of grass species, but are relatively devoid of flowers.

The smooth bark of the Sycamore fig is a source of medicines for chest and glandular treatments, diarrhoea and inflamed throats.

that seedlings of woody plants establish if given a boost of wet years, followed by consecutive years of below average rainfall. The wet years enable the young roots to penetrate deeper soil levels. The dry years that follow suppress the growth of grass that would compete with woody plants for moisture. By this stage, the established woody plants do not need to compete for water as they can extract water from deeper layers beyond the reach of grass roots. The depletion of water from the upper soil levels is normally caused by the over-grazing of livestock and game in small nature reserves with high concentrations of animals. This problem has caused concern in many agriculture areas throughout the world where over-grazing of livestock depletes the grass layer and exposes the topsoil to erosion. If erosion sets in a habitat, the whole process takes an irreversible course, making recovery and rehabilitation of habitats an extremely difficult and quite an expensive process.

Sycamore fig

The sycamore fig is commonly found in the vicinity of water in southern Africa. Its distinguishing characteristics are its trunk, that resembles a collection of pipes, and bright yellow bark. The trunk's structure means that there are many holes and crevices which become inhabited by creatures such as reptiles and rodents. The fruit of the tree is found in clusters on thick branches and attracts insects, birds, fruit bats, vervet monkeys and baboons, while fallen fruit are eaten by warthogs, civets and porcupines. Humans tend to refrain from eating the fruit because they are frequently infested with insects.

The pollination of the flowers of the genus *Ficus* is unique among plants: the flowers of all fig species are enclosed in the fruit, and they are pollinated by a small parasitic wasp, with different wasp species pollinating their own *Ficus* species. A small hole at the apex of the fig allows the wasp to enter. After entering, the winged female wasp lays her eggs. At the same time, the wasp pollinates the flowers with pollen brought from figs that she has previously entered. Small capsules grow around the larvae that feed on the ripening fruit. The wingless males emerge first and pierce a hole through the capsules that envelop females. After mating, the male enlarges the base of the fruit so that the female can emerge in the outside world, and then the male dies. If the fruit is eaten by an animal with the wasps inside, the reproductive cycle cannot be completed. Animals tend to prefer ripening fruits that are rich in sugars. The wasps have developed a mechanism by which there is an accumulation of carbon dioxide inside the fruit while the larvae develop. As a result, the ripening of fruit is inhibited until the female wasp leaves the fruit.

Termites

In many savanna areas in Africa the presence of termites is indicated by their distinctive mounds that rise four to five meters above ground surface. Termites are not ants and belong to a separate order, *Isoptera* – meaning equal wings. (Ants, together with bees, belong to the order *Hymenoptera*). Essentially, termites are sub-terrestrial insects that only rarely expose themselves to daylight. They feed on vegetative material, in particular dead wood, so fulfilling an important function in the cycling of nutrients in savanna ecosystems by depositing the organic matter in their nests and enriching the soil.

Every termite colony contains four different castes, each with a distinctive form and function. The primary reproductive caste, the king and especially the queen, are large and derive from winged individuals. Supplementary reproductive termites are less heavily sclerotized than the primary reproductive caste and appear paler. The third caste, soldiers, are sterile males and females with heavily sclerotized and greatly modified heads with mandibles. The workers are the fourth caste, made up of sterile males and females without special modifications.

The founding of a colony is initiated by the release of large numbers of reproductive termites from the nest soon after the first rains. The release takes place shortly before sunset, so that the termites avoid predation by birds, and is done in synchrony with other ter-

Left:
One of the architectural masterpieces built by termites found in the Sabi-Sand.

mites in the district over a period of several weeks. The termites fly weakly and soon settle and shed their wings. Females attract males by hormones called pheromones. A pair will excavate a small chamber, in which they seal themselves before mating takes place. The female, or queen, starts to lay eggs shortly after mating, although only a few eggs are laid in this period. The royal couple attend the first batch of nymphs, but thereafter nymphs will tend to the succeeding brood. This enables the queen to increase her output of eggs until it reaches a virtually continuous process and she is laying between twenty and thirty thousand eggs per day. A mature colony can include as many as one million termites.

Many insects and other arthropods associate with termites in their nests. These invertebrates have developed special anatomical and physiological features and have adapted to the lifestyle of termites. Some of the arthropods merely feed on nest detritus and debris, while others actively prey on eggs and nymphs.

A butterfly larva.

Opposite:
A carnivorous katydid doing a cleaning job.

Some have intimate symbiotic relationships with the termites, providing food for the termites and in return receiving protection. Among mammals, the aardvark is the most notable for the anatomical adaptations that have enabled it to feed on the plentiful and nutritional food provided by termites. Large carnivores like the aardwolf and the bat-eared fox readily feed on termites when the opportunity arises.

Dung beetles

In the bush, we mostly tend to be attracted to large mammals with their complex behavioral patterns and interactions, yet, observing dung beetles negotiating a dung ball can be just as interesting and rewarding. In southern Africa, diverse conditions mean that there is a variety of dung beetles, which occur in all terrestrial habitat types, from deserts to tropical forests. A number of dung beetle species feed on decaying vegetable matter while others eat carrion. Certain flightless desert-inhabiting species collect and bury vegetable matter and dry dung pellets in moist ground. In turn, the beetles eat the fungus that develops on the decaying matter.

A dung beetle orients itself on top of its ball of dung.

Dung beetles can be classified according to the way in which they treat dung. This varies from simply feeding on it where it falls to complex behavior patterns in which both sexes cooperate in the excavation of tunnels and chambers that they then provision with dung and in which the female lays eggs. Most, however, form dung balls which they then roll walking backwards, using their middle and hind legs to control the ball. They may roll the balls for a considerable distance before burying them in a chamber excavated in the soil. Mating and egg-laying take part after the dung ball is brought to the nest, being used for food for the adults or for protecting the larvae.

When observing dung beetles, one cannot ignore the accompanying fauna. Flies hover on top of the beetles in the hope of laying eggs in the dung ball. Some of the developing larvae may feed on the dung whereas other fly species parasite the brood of dung beetles. Mites are found on the underside of the head and thorax of dung beetles. The mites are predators of fly eggs and use the beetles for transport to dung piles.

The burying of dung has tremendous ecological importance in African savannas as it accelerates nutri-

ent turnover rates, thus facilitating fast and vigorous growth of grass. In some savanna areas, the amount of dung deposited by large herbivorous species makes a substantial contribution of nitrogen to the surface of the soil. Without an agent to transfer the nitrogen to the soils, approximately 80 percent of the nitrogen normally found in the detritus is likely to be lost. In Australia, the introduction of livestock brought about an accumulation of dung and an increase in the densities of fly pests. Dung beetles were considered to be suitable biological agents to combat the reduction of pasture productivity as a result of the accumulation of dung on the surface, and reduce the outbreaks of cattle diseases related to the activity of pest flies. Some of the experiments where particular species of African dung beetles were introduced in farming areas were successful and the need to deploy chemical agents to control the flies was much reduced.

Snakes

Hidden threats are a good source of superstition and myths, and snakes are no exception, especially in Africa. I have seldom met an African who does not detest or is afraid of snakes. The vehicle workshop in the lodge at Sabi-Sand attracted a variety of snakes because it was close to the drain of the water tower which provided a home for frogs and toads, and frequently a snake would be discovered among springs, engine blocks and an old chassis.

Reptiles inhabit a prominent niche in the African savanna. Unlike mammals and birds, snakes and other reptiles can minimize water loss from their bodies and hence may find the desert a comfortable place to live in. Since the metabolic rates of snakes depend on the ambient temperature, snakes do not require to eat frequently, if the temperature is low.

Snakes are predators, though different species have adopted different hunting and killing methods. The mamba is notorious for its virulent poison that can kill

a man within a matter of hours. It is a fascinating snake to observe, although I would not advise approaching it too closely. The mamba is highly mobile and prefers to slide on the branches of a bush than to crawl on the ground. Nonetheless, on the ground the mamba is far from helpless and can reach a speed of 25 kilometers per hour while holding its front part above the ground, although it cannot hold the speed for long distances. The black mamba is particularly aggressive and is a symbol of evil. Whenever I came across a black mamba, the impression of its large, black, beady eyes was hard to forget. Somehow I had a feeling that the snake was doing the same thing that I was – constantly assessing where to go and what to do in the face of danger.

Once I was driving across a bumpy track and came on a large black mamba desperately trying to get off the road. I faced a split-second decision: either to avoid the snake and drive into the bush, where I would risk hitting a log, or to run down the snake and provoke a hostile reaction. I chose the latter, but as we passed the spot where the mamba was, I heard a loud bang on the top panel of the passenger door which the reptile had attacked to defend itself. My assistant, the passenger, was talking to me, not paying attention to the drama that was unfolding. If we had not been in such a tall vehicle, he would certainly have been bitten. When I glanced in the side mirror I saw that the mamba was upright and retracting in haste to avoid the vehicle behind.

A variegated bush snake bloats its throat when threatened.

Left:
Predator turned prey: a burrowing skink, which feeds on insects, is attacked by ants attempting to take advantage of an injury to the skink's head.

99

A giant legless skink heads towards the nearest shelter.

Opposite top:
An African python consumes a scrub hare.

Opposite bottom:
A small African python in a defensive position.

Python

The African python is the longest and probably the strongest of the snakes in Africa. Adult python reach the length of more than seven meters and can kill animals as large as impala. It is widely distributed in forests and wooded savanna areas, and can swim in water with the same ease it moves along the branches of trees. Although its primary killing method is by suffocation, the python first gets hold of its prey by biting it. The python then swiftly curls its body around its prey, suffocating it, and examines the carcass looking for the head by using its sense of smell aided by its forked tongue. Once the head is located, the python rearranges its grip and opens its mouth wide. Using its body to hold the prey, the python pushes the carcass against its mouth, which is built in such a way that the parts of the lower jaw are joined together with strong, flexible tendons. This enables the python to swallow prey larger than the apparent width of its mouth – it can, for example, close its mouth over the horns of an impala ram. When the carcass reaches the front part of the snake's digestive tract, strong muscles are activated which crush the horns, enabling the carcass to slide further down the tract without causing internal injuries. Once it has reached the stomach, the python remains inactive for the duration of the digestion process, which may take weeks to months, depending on the size of prey, the size of python and the ambient conditions, such as temperature and humidity. If dis-

turbed while it is swallowing its prey, a python (which is very vulnerable at this stage) will regurgitate the prey within seconds.

From an evolutionary perspective, pythons are the closest of the snakes to its common ancestor, lizards. Unlike other snakes, they have residual hind legs, which have a function during copulation. Hooks at the end of the small appendages are used to brush against the cloaca, the ventral opening of the digestive tract of the female, which stimulates the female and enables copulation to take place. Also, unlike many other snakes, the female python incubates her eggs. Although cold-blooded, some reptiles have a limited ability to regulate their body temperature, and the female python is able to raise her body temperature to provide favorable conditions for the eggs to develop.

Unfortunately, pythons make valuable artefacts for traditional African medicine and also for witch doctors. This alone is an excellent reason for the decline in pythons throughout their range. In fact, small pythons (the ones that reach Western pet shops) are quite easy to handle, although they can bite. A python bite may indeed have far more serious side effects than that of a poisonous snake due to the fact that they harbor armies of bacteria to help break down swallowed carcasses. Hence, some virulent bacteria strains are found in the mouth of pythons. In addition, pythons have a rather nasty habit of vomiting their stomach contents upon being handled.

Stripe-bellied sand snake

The sand snake is not venomous, although it tends to become aggressive if handled. It is an expert climber and feeds mainly on lizards and frogs, though it may also take small birds and rodents. It is extremely swift moving and can vanish in a gliding motion almost too fast for the eye to follow.

Tree snake (boomslang)

A shy snake that glides silently and gracefully through the branches of trees and shrubs, the tree snake will descend to the ground only in search of food, to bask in the sun or lay eggs. If it is disturbed while on the ground, the snake prefers to climb the nearest tree or bush. The favored diet of the boomslang includes chameleons and lizards, although birds, mice and frogs are also taken. It is highly venomous, even by comparison to the cobra, and has back fangs, which

A Western stripe-bellied sand snake exposes its larynx at the bottom part of its mouth while breathing.

means that prey is firmly held until it is incapacitated by venom, and then swallowed.

I had several encounters with boomslang in Sabi-Sand. Once, as I was reading in my room, I heard something dropping in the bathroom. Thinking that it was the wind, or a vervet monkey playing with something, I continued reading. Then I heard a second noise and went over to investigate. I found a boomslang curled up on the piping of the bath – it had fallen into the bathroom through the open window, probably in hot pursuit of a lizard. It was obviously going to have some trouble getting out the way it had come in as the window was too high and the way up was covered in slippery tiles. Yet without haste, the boomslang moved to the corner below the window, then stretched itself, leaning against the wall. When more than three quarters of its body was vertical on the wall, the boomslang leaned its chin against the window ledge. Then, with amazing agility and skill, it raised the rest of the body and was out of the window in no time.

Mozambique spitting cobra

The Mozambique spitting cobra is among the most common cobra species in southern Africa. It is an omnivorous feeder, taking small mammals, birds, amphibians, lizards and eggs. It has a habit of basking in the sun during cool winter days at the entrance of termite mounds and animal burrows.

The special structure of its fangs enables this cobra to spit its venom. The venom has neuro-toxic effects and is considered second to that of the mamba in its potency. If confronted, the snake rears up as much as two thirds of its total length, spreads its hood and spits in defense, although it can also spit even without elevating its head. The venom is ejected in two directional streams which can reach a distance of two to three meters. Unlike other cobra species, the Mozambique spitting cobra clearly aims its venom at the eyes of its attacker. The whole action is quick and is accomplished with the jaws just parting and the upper lip lifting in a snarl to allow the passage of the venom. The effects of venom hitting the eyes are instantaneous and may cause permanent blindness if not washed out immediately. The amounts of venom released are high and even after discharging several times, the glands appear to replenish rapidly.

The Mozambique spitting cobra can often be found in human settlements in rural areas to which it is attracted in its search for food, and, in fact, came second to the puff adder in the frequency of my encounters with snakes. One of these encounters was a particularly hair-raising experience. I was reading in my room on a hot afternoon when I noticed movement from the corner of my eye. Turning my head towards the door, I saw a cobra sliding into the room and quietly disappearing behind my books that were piled close on the floor. I suspected that it was a spitting cobra and quickly took out my sun glasses for protection. After carefully taking out some of the books, a fully spread hood appeared, although I managed to retreat in time. Not wanting to let this golden opportunity to take a photograph slip by, I closed the door and got my camera and flash, with some dramatic shots of venom in mid-air in mind. Back at the books, the cobra was still waiting for me. With the assistance of a broom, I tried to manipulate the snake into a good position. Instead the cobra retaliated and my lens camera and glasses were covered with the milky venom, but I still could not get a good shot. As a result of all this activity, I was now late for an afternoon game drive with guests. I opened the door and the cobra whisked out. I followed it, but to my horror it slipped underneath the Landrover parked outside. I knocked on the car doors with the broom and pushed it around the internal parts, but the more noise I made, the more the cobra settled in, until it completely disappeared. Patrick, the operation manager, heard the commotion and finally came to my assistance. He proposed we switch on the engine. I did so with the tips of my fingers, revving the engine while standing outside. Nothing happened. Patrick opened the hood and the cobra was there on the top of the radiator cap. Panicking, he slammed the hood and retreated.

When I carefully lifted the hood from the side the cobra darted out, like a flash, and was about to get on to the fender to strike. I was shocked and slammed the hood, jumping backward. While we were still discussing what to do the snake suddenly disappeared.

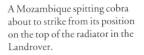

A Mozambique spitting cobra about to strike from its position on the top of the radiator in the Landrover.

Yellow-billed oxpeckers are habitually found around buffaloes, which supply them with ample food gathering opportunities.

Oxpecker

In southern Africa, there are two species of oxpecker, the yellow-billed and the red-billed. The distribution range of both species includes the eastern regions of southern Africa, although the red-billed oxpecker is less common than its counterpart. Oxpeckers are often seen standing on the backs of large herbivores, with which they have a special relationship – they relieve their hosts of parasites and provide an early warning system; in return, the hosts provide food for the oxpeckers. The birds live in flocks of six to ten individuals that feed together on rhino, giraffe, buffalo, sable, wildebeest, kudu, zebra and impala.

Related to the starling, oxpeckers have short legs with strong, curved talons to grip the fur of herbivores. They are helped in this by the fact that their middle digit is shorter than their rear one, which is unusual among song birds. Their beak is wide and powerful and has a larger lower than upper part. The wings are long and narrow which allow fast flying and high maneuverability. The tail feathers are sturdy and carry the body weight while foraging.

Although oxpeckers fulfill important functions for herbivores, they are also a pest as they can peck at open wounds, sometimes aiding in the transfer of diseases. Oxpeckers are also capable of expanding existing wounds for the purpose of attracting insects that may serve as additional food supply.

Francolin

Francolins are siblings of the pheasant family, the African counterparts to the Asian chukar and the American partridge. They are typical savanna birds with distinctive plumage on their breast and belly. One of the main characteristics of francolins, experienced by many visitors to African wilderness areas, are their sharp, loud calls during the early morning hours.

Nests are built on the ground, hidden in grass. Chicks will leave the nest and follow the hen shortly after hatching – as such, they are termed precocious

A Swainson's francolin.

A red-billed francolin declares its territory.

Opposite:
A male black-bellied korhaan in territorial display.

primaries and dropping to the ground with their wings held over their back.

The black-bellied korhaan prefers short grass savannas that allow approaching predators to be detected. Another important reason for the preference for this kind of habitat is that its diet consists mainly of insects, including dung beetles, grasshoppers, caterpillars, crickets and mantises which thrive in these surroundings. The black-bellied korhaan is found in pairs, and eggs are laid on the bare ground among grass stalks.

Red-crested korhaan

Among the bustard family, the red-crested korhaan has the most spectacular courtship displays. During these displays, the male's red crest, which is normally hidden beneath dull brown head plumage, is erected. The male takes off almost vertically, reaching a height of approximately fifteen meters before he tumbles over and drops straight to the ground. Just as he is about to crash to the ground, he spreads his wings and glides away for some distance before landing.

The red-crested korhaan is a common species of woodland savannas and may be found in patchy habitats of thick scrub and open areas. Unlike many members of the bustard family, this bird is a fast flier that dashes away at high speed, flying for the safety of trees. However, it also relies heavily on its camouflage and will stand motionless waiting for danger to pass.

Hornbill

Hornbills are common members of animal communities in semi-arid savannas. They are large birds with huge bills which have razor-sharp edges and sometimes also an appendage on top, giving the bird a peculiar appearance. However, despite the formidable look and strength of the bills, they are very lightweight. The birds are noisy, particularly when flying. Their flight is heavy and the movement of their wings creates a whistling sound.

Hornbills generally nest in tree holes. In most species, the female enters the nest and seals the entrance with mud. She later creates a hatch through which the male inserts food while the female incubates the eggs. The female remains confined for approximately three months, during which time she keeps her nest clean and disposes of excrement and leftover food through the hatch. The female molts all her feathers during the incubation period and leaves the nest only after a new coat of feathers has grown, assisting the male in finding food for the young. The young seal the enlarged entrance of the nest after the departure of the female without outside assistance.

animals, needing little or no assistance at all. The red-billed francolin lives in pairs or in groups of up to twenty birds. They run for cover if disturbed and fly reluctantly. Francolins feed on seeds, fallen grain, shoots, leaves, berries and insects.

Black-bellied korhaan

The black-bellied korhaan is smaller than the Kori bustard but larger than the black korhaan. Unlike its counterparts, this korhaan dwells in high-rainfall habitats. It is a relatively tame bird that can be easily approached and photographed. The male is particularly photogenic during the breeding season – they choose a prominent place on the ground to display, and reaching high with their long neck, call as they reach the full height of their posture. Flight displays are also spectacular with males showing off their white

Ground hornbill

Ground hornbills are in many respects exceptional members of the hornbill family. As their name suggests, they are more terrestrial than other members of the family, and hunt for insects, frogs, small reptiles and mammals, even on occasion killing and eating large snakes. They are usually found in pairs or small family parties, hunting independently while keeping each other within sight. Their call is a deep booming sound, although males and females have different tones. This is mostly heard at the first sign of dawn, but subsides as day breaks.

At sunset, ground hornbills retire to roost on tall trees. Because of their size, however, they sometimes have difficulty in finding a sufficiently large hole in the tree, and may compromise and nest in a rock crevice. Unlike other hornbills, the ground hornbill does not seal the entrance to its nest with mud. The male feeds the female while she incubates her eggs but may also take turns assisting in the incubation process. Other hornbills, such as mature siblings, may help in raising the young.

Hamerkop

A common resident of inland waters, the hamerkop is the smallest member of the stork family. It ventures to arid regions following the appearance of rainwater pools, where it searches for tadpoles, small insects and other invertebrates. While foraging, the hamerkop wades in or around shallow water, although it can also fly slowly over water and snatch food from the surface of the water with its bill.

The nest of the hamerkop is a huge oven-shaped mass of sticks that is set on the base of forked branches, a cliff or a rock in the river. It contains breeding chambers coated with dry mud and weighs about 50 kilograms. The nest is constructed by two separate mating couples and may take six months to complete, although material is added to their nest constantly.

Though small, the hamerkop does share many characteristics with the larger birds of the stork family, such as the marabou, spoonbill, cattle egret and the ibis. Storks tend to dwell in the vicinity of water sources but are adapted to semi-aquatic lives. They have relatively long legs and a variety of bill forms

A ground hornbill collects insects. The couple raise their young and feed them a variety of insects and small reptiles.

A hammerkop, the smallest of the stork family, fishes along the Sabie River.

Opposite:
The long eyelashes of the ground hornbill are not hairs but hair-like feathers.

Blue-eared starlings are gregarious birds that frequent camp sites in search for scraps of food.

The grey lourie, also called the "go away bird" because of its distinct call, is a common bird of the Bushveld throughout southern Africa.

Opposite:
A male bateleur eagle.

depending on their preferred food-type, which includes fish, amphibians, lizards, snakes, insects and other invertebrates. Food gathering is assisted by the shape of the neck that can be extended by using a very strong and elastic tendon. Their method of hunting involves striking prey with their bill as the head is launched forward accurately at high speed.

Bateleur

Not only does the bateleur have the most colorful appearance among eagles in the southern African savannas, but it also has the most impressive pattern of flight. Its name in French implies an acrobat or tightrope walker, which refers to its inflight action of rocking from side to side, rarely flapping its wings as it glides. While sexual dimorphism is not pronounced among eagle species, there is a distinct difference in the color of male and female bateleurs, with the primary flying feathers of the male being much darker than those of the female. The wings of the bateleur are long and pointed and the tail is very short. This allows the bateleur to soar confidently at great speed at relatively low heights between strong, hot air thermals. The aerobatic maneuvers it performs with only slight

movements of its wings are breathtaking. In particular, its flight displays during courtship involve a couple performing coordinated maneuvers, rolling, looping and holding each others' talons in midair. These rituals may last for hours.

The bateleur can scan an extensive area while searching for its favorite prey – usually reptiles, small mammals and carrion. Its nest is usually built on the top branches of an acacia tree, a relatively small structure onto which material is added each year as the couple returns to breed. Eagles are territorial and will jealously guard their territory against rivals, particularly during the breeding season. Because of this, it is unusual to see more than a couple of eagles in any one spot. Bateleurs, however, can be seen in small groups which include siblings that have not yet established their own territories.

Like many other eagle species, the female bateleur lays one egg, although it is capable of laying an additional egg in case the original is infertile or lost. The male feeds the female for more than a month while she attends the egg. Three months after hatching, the chick is ready to leave the nest, although it returns occasionally for long periods after fledging.

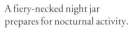

A fiery-necked night jar prepares for nocturnal activity.

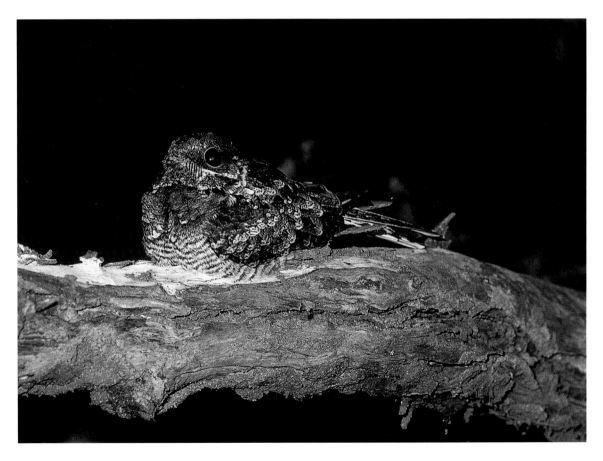

A spotted eagle owl.

Owls

Most bird species are diurnal – mostly because the activity of flying requires good orientation and fast reactions, and, in addition, birds need to see details to survive. Owls, however, have adapted to conditions of poor light and are not only able to maintain their orientation, but can also catch prey. Commonly, owls settle at prominent observation posts at dusk, when their main prey species, such as rodents, small reptiles and amphibians, start their nocturnal activities. For a long time, researchers believed that owls found their way in the dark through superior vision. Indeed, most owl species have large eyes positioned in the front of the face that provide them with good binocular vision for estimating distances. They also have high concentrations of rod cells that are sensitive to light on the retina, providing the owl with a reasonable picture in a dark night. However, the hearing of these nocturnal birds is highly developed and this ability primarily enables the owl to pinpoint its prey. The exterior parts of an owl's ears are non-symmetrical. Hence, sounds that reach the ears do not arrive quite at the same time, despite the small distance between the ears. The owl can distinguish different sounds and locate their origin, turning its head toward the direction of the source of sound and focusing on the location. The owl can also rotate its head without moving its body, thus remaining silent. In addition, owls are silent fliers. Their body is covered with a soft plumage that cushions sudden movements and reduces the surface resistance to the flow of air, while their primary flight feathers have hairs in the shape of a comb that help silence the movement of the wings while flying. The resultant reduction in flight capacity does not hinder their ability to catch prey in any way.

When it comes to getting a grip on their prey, owls are equipped with formidable talons. Owls swallow their prey, although some parts, such as bones, hair, feathers and bills are not digested; these parts are separated and packed in the stomach, to be vomited in the form of scats within hours of swallowing.

Spotted eagle owl

One of the most common owl species in southern Africa, the spotted eagle owl, occupies a variety of habitats ranging from deserts to forests. During the day it rests on branches of tall trees or amongst rocks, emerging at dusk and settling on vantage points. It feeds on mice, moles, rats, shrews, lizards, insects and birds. Their favorite nesting sites include cliffs, old mines and hollow trees. In the deserts it may nest on top of a weaver nest.

Scops owls are small and highly camouflaged birds which are heard at night more often than they are seen.

The king of the hill. A white-backed vulture asserts its dominance on top of a zebra carcass.

Following pages:
Whitebacked vultures confronting each other on the top of a giraffe carcass in the Sabi-Sand.

Vultures

The African savannas littered with an endless supply of fresh carcasses left over from the kills by the larger predators, such as lions and leopards, are an ideal habitat for vultures, the flying scavengers. Aggregations of a variety of vulture species around carcasses can reach hundreds of birds, and, indeed, the number of vultures is an indication of the size of the carcass and its stage of decomposition. The more vultures, the more likely it is to be a large, fresh carcass.

Vultures specialize in carrion meat and, therefore, serve a vital function in the cycling of nutrients in savanna ecosystems. Vultures and other scavengers like hyenas and jackals facilitate the decomposition process by dismembering and digesting large quantities of meat that otherwise would take considerable time to be absorbed by the soil and subsequently nourish plant life. In addition, they also help prevent large accumulations of pest, flies and around decomposing carcasses.

From the early hours of the morning, once the warm rays of the sun have heated the ground, vultures take off. Using hot air thermals to gain height, they glide and scan the savanna below for carcasses. Vultures are sensitive to changes in wind directions and in the right atmospheric conditions can reach considerable heights. While scanning the ground, a vulture will also keep a vigilant lookout for other vultures. If one bird detects a carcass, it folds its wings and dives towards the ground. Other vultures in the vicinity, that see this, will follow, and thus a quiet scene where a cheetah, for example, is resting beside a freshly killed impala, can suddenly become a noisy confrontation between vultures falling like stones from the sky and the cheetah attempting to salvage the carcass. Like other confrontations in the savanna, size and numbers determine the outcome. A cheetah can be easily chased off a kill by a group of more than ten vultures. However, a pride of lions will not give way to such an intrusion and will stalk vultures that dare to come too close to a carcass.

The ability to detect a kill from considerable distances is attributed to the superb eyesight of the vulture. Raptors have two major nerve cell concentrations on the retina layer of the eye that enhance the resolution of distant objects. Each eye can independently cover a wide angle of sight. In addition, the range of overlap between the eyes, the binocular range (which is shared with humans), allows for three-dimensional sight and provides the ability to estimate distances and shapes.

Once a large carcass has been detected, a variety of vulture species swarm onto the scene. An intense con-frontation ensues between the birds as they attempt to reach the softer parts of the carcass. The squawking and hissing of vultures appear very aggressive, although confrontations are mostly between vultures of the same species and inter-species competition for food is rare as each one tends to specialize on different food items. For example, the largest of the African vultures, the lappet-faced vulture, feeds on skin parts, tendons and muscles. With its powerful beak the vulture is able to easily cut through the skin of large herbivores, often allowing other vultures access to softer parts of the carcass. The whitebacked vulture and whitefaced vulture normally make up the majority of the vultures around a carcass. These birds opt for the inner parts and organs – having bare necks they run no risk of soiling any difficult-to-clean feathers, when they insert their heads deep into the carcass and probe for food. The smaller vulture species, such as the Egyptian vulture and the hooded vulture, feed on the scraps left behind by larger vultures. Their small, slender beaks allow them to clean the last remains of the carcass delicately.

Aggression between vultures can be correlated to their hunger level. A hungry vulture is likely to repel a well-nourished companion on a carcass. Vultures that have satisfied their appetites will retire a few meters away from the carcass where they are less likely to be harassed. A vulture can consume about half its body weight in food, and in some cases finds considerable difficulty in taking off after a good feast. While waiting for food to digest, a vulture will spend time cleaning itself of scraps and ensure that its feathers are in a pristine condition for flying.

Serious confrontation erupts as vultures scramble to feed on the remains of a giraffe that was killed by lions.

Vervet monkey

Visitors to wooded camp sites in southern Africa can expect to meet vervet monkeys. Any affection towards the monkeys quickly changes to exasperation as they raid precious food stores. Generally, the primates are opportunistic omnivores that feed on seeds, fruits, pods, leaves, flowers, insects and even lizards and small birds. In their search for insects, vervet monkeys may turn over logs, branches and dung on the ground. They may also bite acacia and other trees to generate the flow of sap which they then lick.

Vervet monkeys live in hierarchical troops. While females stay in their natal family, males emigrate as they near maturity, and the social ranking of individuals is determined according to the mother's rank. Individuals with lower social ranking will groom with one another or take care of infants belonging to individuals of superior ranking. As a result, the offspring of a high-ranking female have a better chance of survival at times of food shortage, as the female has better access to food sources. Although males dominate females of similar social ranking, this can be rebuffed by a temporary coalition formed by females.

Social interactions are supplemented with tactile communication. Social grooming is quite frequent and extremely important in the maintenance of kinship and other bonds. Being groomed is clearly a pleasurable experience. Even if not reciprocated, grooming can be socially rewarding. It offers ways for lower-ranking animals to approach and make friendly contacts with dominant individuals. Juvenile and adult females that want to handle an infant may gain access to the baby by grooming its mother. Since grooming is very soothing, mothers may distract their offspring by grooming them during aggressive phases of weaning. Similarly, the aggression of a male toward a troop member is diverted through grooming. Playing also has social functions, as opposed to carnivores that use it to learn hunting methods. Infants may start playing two weeks after birth, while adults may briefly play with juveniles.

Most breeding is monopolized by dominant males. Female vervet monkeys, however, tend to play a prominent part during territorial disputes with neighboring troops. Males will take an active role in a dispute only if females of their troop are threatened

Social bonds among vervet-monkeys are a cornerstone in the organization of the group.

Opposite:
A vervet monkey submits itself to the grooming performed by a troop mate.

by foreign males. Low-ranking males will readily transfer to other troops in the hope of improving their social and reproductive status. Young males may endure a relative long period of harassment by adult males until they manage to cultivate relationships with a neighboring troop to which they transfer. However, immigrant males face the possibility of serious injuries by females of the receiving troop. Since male vervet monkeys are not able to live a solitary life, the period of transfer and admission into a new troop is critical. Males may also form small coalitions within the troop and transfer together.

Vervet monkeys are vulnerable to savanna predators such as leopards and eagles because of their small size and also because of the fact that they forage in relatively open areas. As a result, vervet monkeys seldom venture out more than several hundred meters from a wooded area. For observers in the field the conspicuous bark of vervet monkeys is a sure indication that a leopard is prowling in the vicinity. Vervet monkeys also respond to alarm calls of birds, such as francolins and guinea fowl.

Tree squirrel

Tree squirrels are predominantly vegetarian and may eat insects to supplement their diet during certain periods of the year. They commonly eat flowers, leaves, seeds, berries, fruit and the bark of a wide range of trees and shrubs. They spend most of their time in trees and display considerable agility when feeding – by hanging with their hind feet on small branches to reach for food. The tree squirrel will also cache hard food such as seeds and nuts, digging a small hole where they place their food, then covering the hole and packing the soil back using their nose. Cache sites are carefully chosen and individual squirrels take great care that other members of the group do not see them. Nonetheless, some group members seem to be quite observant because food stealing is still quite common.

Tree squirrels are diurnal, being most active in the morning and late afternoon, thus avoiding the hottest hours of the day. They bask in the sun, particularly after emerging from their nest on cool winter mornings. Grooming is an important aspect of their behavior: the young are forcibly groomed by the mothers who pin them down with their front legs. Tree squirrels are usually observed alone, although they maintain pair bonds and the female may be seen with her young. Groups comprising of a breeding pair and sub-adult squirrels are common. Individual recognition is through the olfactory sense, as squirrels will acquire the same smell in the nest through mutual

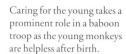
Caring for the young takes a prominent role in a baboon troop as the young monkeys are helpless after birth.

Good morning bushveld. A bush squirrel stretches in the early hours of the morning.

Opposite:
A bush squirrel on a vantage point warming itself on a cool winter day.

grooming or marking with the anal glands. Strangers are chased not only from the entrance to the nesting hole but also from feeding grounds.

Their nests are either natural holes or those made by woodpeckers, and are lined with grasses and leaves. The nests are occasionally cleaned and the cover may be replaced. Young are born at any time of the year although a breeding peak occurs during the summer months. Like the ground squirrel, babies are altricial – born helpless. They can get out of the entrance to the nest by the end of their third week, but stay close to the adult female until they are about a month old. The females are very attentive to their young and remain in the nest constantly for the first three days after birth. The male remains with the family throughout the period when offspring are brought up. Ground squirrels become sexually mature by the age of ten months.

Groups establish territories that are defended by the males. The territory is marked by scent through the anal glands, mouth wiping and urination. The male routinely maintains the freshness of the scent marking, although the intensity of marking increases upon the appearance of strangers.

Having a wide range of predators including eagles, owls, snakes, and mammalian carnivores, tree squirrels need to be vigilant to avoid their predators. They are most vulnerable when foraging in the open. They are very cautious when on the ground and will move with abrupt movements, stopping and looking every few steps, with the tail erect and twitching. Upon a sign of danger, tree squirrels dash for the safety of the nesting hole or a tree trunk. On other occasions they will mob predators, with all the members of a group making loud clicking calls accompanied by much tail flicking as they take up a prominent and safe vantage point beyond the reach of the predator. As the predator gets nearer, the intensity of calls increases. Individual squirrels respond in a similar manner upon the sight of a particular kind of predator. The vigilance of squirrels is a useful early warning system in the daily life at camp. The excitement of the squirrells' alarm call can mean a snake is on its way towards the kitchen hut or to one of the tents.

Dwarf mongoose

This small and agile mongoose is commonly found on termite mounds in savanna habitats. It feeds on larval beetles, termites, crickets, grasshoppers and small vertebrates like lizards and birds. Dwarf mongooses are gregarious animals that live in packs dominated by a mated pair that produce all the offspring. Siblings and unrelated pack members help to raise the young, and although this seems altruistic, immigrants of both sexes stand a fair chance of becoming dominant and producing their own offspring. Upon reaching dominant status, a pair can maintain its status for several years. Males disperse more than females and wander further away from the pack, but as a result the mortality rate of males is higher than that of females.

Dwarf mongoose live in highly cooperative societies with well-developed social roles and genial relationships within the pack. Pack members nibble, groom and scent mark one another. The alpha pair seldom expresses their dominance, except during breeding activities. Although females other than the alpha female may produce offspring, they soon disappear, and it may be that the alpha female practices infanticide. Members of the pack help to feed the young and also guard and groom them, but the alpha female remains the leader of the pack, initiating the daily activities such as emerging from the burrows and foraging. The male takes the burden of guarding, assisted by sub-adult males. Most of his time is spent at the top of the den looking out for potential danger.

A group of dwarf mongoose performs mutual grooming. Beyond the functional purpose of this behavior, it enhances social bonds and hierarchy.

Each pack has its own territory. Should a larger pack meet a smaller one, an attempt to overtake the smaller pack's mound is likely to succeed. Generally, however, encounters between packs result in each pack withdrawing back to the center of its own territory. Within their territory, dwarf mongoose can be seen associating with birds such as the drongo, lilac-breasted roller and hornbills, which also feed on insects. The drongo and the roller rely on the mongoose to flush insects that they in turn catch, while hornbills forage with the mongoose, to the extent that they compete for the same food. Nonetheless, the mongoose benefit immensely from the alarm calls hornbills make when they spot predators.

Dwarf mongoose communicate mainly through sound and smell. They favor areas with high ground and bush cover. As a result, contact between pack members during foraging is difficult through the curtain of vegetation. This has led to the development of a complex and extensive array of calls, and most activities have a different type of vocalization. In addition, the rate of calling increases as a particular activity intensifies. The call mongoose make while they forage, a peep emitted every three seconds, is quite familiar to observers in the field. However, if an observer moves abruptly in the vehicle, the mongoose suddenly emit a panic twitter and dash for cover. Smell is also important and dwarf mongoose have cheek and anal glands that produce and emit a pungent smell. They rub the paste onto objects, sex partners and offspring.

For the dwarf mongoose, individual vigilance is important for survival even when living in groups.

Spotted hyena

The spotted hyena has very little appeal to visitors when encountered in the bush. Heavily built, with well-developed front legs and shoulders, as well as a massive jaw, hyenas are physically adapted to scavenging, carrying carcasses over long distances and crushing heavy bones. However, a more detailed observation reveals that the spotted hyena is a highly gregarious carnivore which has intricate and fascinating social interactions. Typically, in areas where food is scarce or comprised of small prey, the spotted hyena is solitary. Foraging singly, the hyena prefers to scavenge or prey on old and sick animals or helpless young of large mammals. In areas where food is abundant, spotted hyenas form clans that hunt cooperatively as well as singly.

Females dominate the clans as they are bigger and more aggressive than males. Aggressiveness is determined by male sex hormones, especially testosterone, and the masculine development of females starts at an early age because of elevated androgen concentrations in their blood. The presence of a male phallus in female spotted hyenas may be a by-product of this process, and in the field, it takes quite some time to distinguish between the sexes – the best criteria are size and aggression levels, rather than the features of the genitals.

Although hyenas may live in communal systems, the females take care of their young. Competition replaces cooperation. As a result, access to kills, mating opportunities, and emigration of males out of the clan depend on the ability to dominate and establish a position high on the pecking order of the clan. The competition for food is particularly fierce for mothers that need to nurture their young. Young spotted hyenas suckle for a year and a half, and so the production of milk is quite an important factor in the survival of the young. The volume and duration of milk production are probably linked to the percantage of bone in the diet.

Female dominance is asserted on almost all occasions when there is a question of precedence. The females are also the ones that lead the clan in territorial boundary marking excursions and territorial fights. Although they do not have precedence over females, males establish their own dominance order. Males born in the clan abstain from reproductive competition, and only immigrant males participate in mating. Among this group, the male that dominates the rest also monopolizes mating with clan females.

Hierarchy is also passed down to the next generation. The offspring of high-ranking females have a better chance of survival as they eat better and grow faster and bigger. The alpha female is able to claim

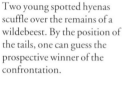

Two young spotted hyenas scuffle over the remains of a wildebeest. By the position of the tails, one can guess the prospective winner of the confrontation.

the largest share of the prey and allows her cubs to share in the spoils. Bonds between mothers and daughters stay while the daughters remain in the clan, whereas males emigrate when they mature. Hence, it is likely that sons of high-ranking females will acquire dominance in another clan as they are both larger and have much more confidence than low-ranking males. Because of the nature of the structure of clans, males that achieve an alpha ranking have a tremendous genetic payoff. Given a three-year tenure in a sizable clan, a male can sire dozens of offspring.

The focus of activity within a clan territory is the communal den. This is a mound of bare ground or a small cave in a rocky outcrop, often identified by beaten paths in the grass and the remains of carcasses. Most dens are used for generations by different species, although hyenas rarely stay at one den for more than a few months before moving on. Although adult hyenas stay in the proximity of the den, males do not play a paternal role and few, if any, are allowed to approach the cubs.

Spotted hyenas are highly opportunistic predators. They rely on their excellent eyesight and hearing to detect handicapped animals. Typically, they will approach a herd of ungulate boldly and scan the fleeing animals in an attempt to find stragglers. When hunting, hyenas depend on their stamina during the chase. Hyenas may run for several kilometers at a constant speed and bring their intended prey to a state of exhaustion. This is a common technique on the plains of the East African savannas, but in southern Africa, where dense bush may obstruct the view of prey, hyenas rely more on the element of surprise and confusion. They may also concentrate on animals that are highly territorial, such as impala rams during the rut season. The rams are reluctant to leave their territory and hyenas normally manage to corner them at some stage during the chase. In Savuti, warthogs are a favorite prey. Hyenas block their retreat to their burrows and take advantage of the ensuing confusion.

Cooperative hunting is necessary to counteract the opposition of prey. For example, a stallion zebra might stage a determined defense of a harem of females and their foals. Through a common effort, hyenas distract and challenge the stallion while the rest go for the foals. Although females usually lead communal hunting, more males than females participate in the hunt.

Hyenas bite at the legs or belly of their prey, or grip the tail. Once the prey is pinned down, other hyenas arrive and the victim is usually disemboweled and dies within minutes. Small prey is usually grabbed

by the neck and shaken. Most prey do not attempt to resist and are probably in a state of shock or exhaustion by the time they are pulled down. Although cooperation during the phases of hunting is low, aggression between individuals is minimal when the prey is devoured. Instead of fighting over their share like lions, hyenas compete by eating as much as possible as quickly as they can. Hyenas can gulp down about a third of their body weight, compared to lions, who can consume only a quarter of their body weight.

Competition with other predators is a key factor in determining the success and size of hyena clans. Second to the lion, the spotted hyena is the largest African predator. Since they share the same prey species, competition arises in areas where large herbivores are abundant, and cooperation among members

By the age of two months, spots are apparent through the black coat of hyena cubs. At this early age the social status of the cubs is influenced by the social rankings of its parents.

of a hyena clan is important to outrank and deter lions. Hyenas go as far as to distract lions from their kills, thus risking getting killed or maimed by the lions. Nonetheless, through their numerical advantage, hyenas harass lions and compel them to abandon their kills. Regular disputes between hyenas and lions occur in the savuti area. Sometimes hyenas manage to drive away the lions, to the extent that lions must climb trees to avoid harm. At other times, hyenas are at a disadvantage and are forced to retreat, much to their frustration. Mature male lions are seldom deterred by hyenas, no matter how numerous they are. If lions hear the victory chorus and whooping frenzy following a successful kill by hyenas, they rush to the scene to grab their share.

Since spotted hyenas are highly opportunistic creatures, their curiosity and ability to learn and improvise are not to be underestimated. Hyenas may cause damage to equipment with soft parts like rubber tires and plastic bowls, particularly if traces of food or fat are left on them. In the Savuti camp, hyenas grabbed soap wherever they could get it, even from inside tents. I used to leave the flap of the tent open, knowing that at some time hyenas or leopards would investigate the inside. Whenever hyenas came in, they headed directly towards the wash bag where the soap was. If, however, I moved slightly, the hyenas would dart outside. Knowing that hyenas used to prowl singly or in pairs in the camp made such an invitation a little less dangerous.

Hyenas became a nuisance at the Savuti camp, as anything left unprotected would have their teeth marks on them the next morning. At one stage, a bold young male was shot after he persistently tried to enter the tent of my colleagues who had their two small daughters inside. Nonetheless, knowing their habits, it was not difficult to reach a state of coexistence. One night, I was woken up by the whoop and shrill sounds of hyenas at the camp premises. There was a lot of growling and, obviously, a clan dispute was taking place. Gradually, the sounds grew louder and closer. Within minutes, the tent was surrounded by the flurry of hyenas dashing around, throwing columns of dust in the air. In the midst of the turmoil I noticed that the clan was mobbing a male that had recently joined the clan. Evidently, he was not welcome and the clan was going to teach him a hard lesson. Knowing that I was inside the tent, the male pressed against the tent, covering his back and flanks. The sound was horrific. Only at such close quarters does one realize the power of these creatures. I moved towards the exit and came to the defense of the male. Once my silhouette

appeared at the entrance of the tent, the clan retreated instantly, howling. The severely beaten male looked at me sheepishly and then disappeared in the opposite direction. I never saw him again.

Being highly social creatures, hyenas have developed a very complex communication and behavior repertoire. Observing hyenas interacting can be a far more interesting pastime in the African bush than watching lions, who, after all, spend most of their time sleeping and resting. The greeting ceremony of hyenas is highly ritualized. Whenever two individuals come together, they sniff each other's mouth and head, then nose each other's phallus by lifting the leg closest to the companion.

Another behavior pattern that involves olfactory communication is pasting. Spotted hyenas routinely mark tall grass stalks with their anal glands. While pasting, hyenas adopt a unique posture with the tail curled over the back and the phallus extended. They excrete a soapy secretion on the grass stalks that marks the boundaries of the territories or, when used within the home range, to indicate their presence to other hyenas. Stools are another distinctive kind of territory marking, as bone residues in the hyenas' diet cause their scats to turn chalky white when they dry and make the stools more conspicuous. Like many other canids, hyenas may even wallow in the fresh dung that large mammals leave behind. The new and con-

spicuous smell on their fur is quite a source of attraction to other hyenas and attracts additional attention from other members of the clan.

The call of the spotted hyena is highly distinctive and can be carried over extensive distances. Like lions, hyenas use calls to establish or maintain contact to other members of the clan. Presumably, hyenas can distinguish between individuals by the tone of the calls. Visitors to the African bush who stay long enough can distinguish the various hyena calls and predict the situation that leads to particular sounds. This comes in handy when trying to locate the sites of new kills, or find a confrontation between lions and hyenas. However, the observer should expect to stay up for almost

Though a skilled hunter, the body of the spotted hyaena is perfectly adapted for handling carcasses. Their powerful jaw enables hyaena to crush large bones and the taller upper torso allows the hyaena to carry a carcass.

the entire night as hyenas are mostly active during the hours after sunset and before the sun rises.

Young hyenas are quite playful and, in fact, participate in the usual chase and fight games that resemble the hunting techniques of adults. Females often play with the cubs and sometimes even males are allowed to come closer to the den to take part in the games. Curiosity plays a prominent role in shaping individual characteristics and establishing future rank in the clan. Hyena cubs may at times approach vehicles and investigate beneath them, or chew the rubber bumper. Cubs may also approach people when they enjoy the safety of the nearby den. However, the curious approach of cubs is replaced by fear as the hyena matures. In general, hyenas fear man. On the other hand, the advantage of numbers while in a clan may supersede this, and hence hyenas can be quite dangerous. Although human casualties are rather rare and mostly confined to unattended babies and infants, injuries from hyenas are quite common. In areas where large predators are seldom seen and people choose to sleep on the ground in the open without any protection, prowling hyenas have been known to nibble and bite at peoples' noses and ears.

Cheetah

The cheetah is a specialist carnivore which captures its prey – small- and medium-sized antelope – due to its superior speed when chasing. It is easily distinguished from other cats by its distinctive spot markings (as opposed to the blotches of the leopard), a loose and rangy build, a small head, high-set eyes and small ears. It is the fastest land mammal and has a top speed of about 90 to 100 kilometers per hour, which it attains thanks to the evolutionary development of long limbs, a highly flexible spine, and claws that only half retract, providing additional traction during rapid acceleration. However, cheetahs lack stamina and require to overtake their prey and pounce within 300 meters of beginning the chase.

The favorite prey of cheetah in southern Africa include impala, springbok, duikers, bushbuck and warthog. Cheetahs may also prey on juveniles of large herbivore species such as roan, sable and wildebeest, but mostly they avoid prey larger than themselves. In acquiring the speed to catch fast antelopes, the cheetah has compromised strength, body mass and weaponry for lightness, long limbs and small teeth. Being light and frail, cheetahs may sustain injury

while attempting to pull down large prey, whereas other cats, such as leopard and lion, with heavier, more compact bodies can pin down and overwhelm their prey relatively easily.

The cheetah is essentially a hunter on the open plains and relies primarily on sight to track its prey. As such, it is diurnal and may be seen in groups. However, the cheetah is not really a social mammal and these groups consist mostly of a mother and her sub-adult cubs or a small male coalition. The reasons for the formation of coalitions remain somewhat enigmatic. Unlike lions, where prey abundance and kinship provide good criteria for forming groups, female cheetahs are solitary, and males that meet females in estrus may have exclusive mating rights. The formation of coalitions commonly originates with litter mates that stay together after separating from their mother.

While in groups, social relations between cheetah males are restrained. Visual communication provides important cues for social interactions. The "tear lines" on the face of the cheetah have been a source of much speculation among experts. It seems that the lines help to transmit different facial expressions that represent different moods, as well as disguising the outline of the head when the cheetah faces a potential prey.

Body contact is minimal and the only form of social interaction is head-rubbing. Nonetheless, males jointly mark and defend their territory. It is likely that with coalitions that are bigger than the common two-adult group, prey size may also increase. The group uses their combined might to overpower and pull down prey as large as sub-adult wildebeest. However, cheetah also feed on much smaller mammals.

Cheetahs are attractive animals to observe when they are searching for prey. A cheetah actively hunting walks around with a measured pace and an alert expression on its face. It may utilize termite mounds and trees with low branches as vantage points. Depending on the characteristics of its prey, the cheetah may choose different strategies to approach the prey. With impala, for example, the cheetah prefers a stealthy approach, or remains under cover and waits for the herd to close before it starts its chase. If, however, a juvenile wildebeest is the intended prey, the cheetah may approach the herd openly. The wildebeest will respond by approaching the cheetah to get a closer look. The purpose of the approach in the open is to select the intended prey and manipulate the herd into a position from which it will be easier to close in on the quarry. In East Africa, where herds are scat-

tered over the open plains, the cheetah may flush an unsuspecting herd and take advantage of the confusion to pounce on a quarry from another herd.

Although the cheetah is considered an efficient hunter, only about half of its attempts to take prey are successful. The most common reason for this failure is early detection by the prey. Cheetahs do not take wind direction into account when stalking, and unlike hyenas, cheetahs do not attempt to single out handicapped or sick individuals.

In the chase, however, the acceleration of a cheetah can be breathtaking to observe. As its quarry changes its position rapidly during the course of the chase, the cheetah prefers to slow down so that it can follow the movements of the intended prey. For that purpose, the cheetah uses its long, flat tail which moves like a steering rudder from side to side and provides a counterbalance to the body. When it overtakes its quarry, the cheetah tries to unbalance the prey by striking the rump, thigh or hind leg with its forepaw. The victim crashes to the ground and may break a leg in the process. Using two legs and its chest, the cheetah pins the prey to the ground and grips on the windpipe, usually from behind to avoid the

A female and her grown cubs examine and mark a termite mound.

137

hooves. Since the canines of the cheetahs are small, it has to use an accurate and a vice-like grip to stop the prey struggling too much. A cheetah's small upper canine teeth have roots adjacent to the nasal passages which allow increased air intake and enable the cheetah to maintain its grip on the prey and suffocate it.

The chase takes a tremendous amount of energy from the cheetah. It is not surprising, therefore, that following a chase the cheetah needs to rest and cool down for about half an hour before resuming hunting attempts or feeding. However, if the prey was overtaken in an open area with little cover, the cheetah must drag the carcass to a safer position so that other predators and scavengers cannot interfere with its feeding. A female with cubs has much more to accomplish. Not only is the mother required to drag the carcass to cover so that the cubs and meat are undetected, but also the frequency of her hunting has to increase dramatically to meet the requirements of the cubs.

The cheetah is outranked by all large African carnivores, and is likely to sustain injury in every confrontation. Such confrontation may have disastrous effects on the future hunting ability of the cheetah, and so, if another large predator approaches, such as

lion or spotted hyena, the cheetah will give way without a fight. A female with cubs may resist giving up a kill longer, but if the approaching predator persists, the cheetah will retreat and abandon the kill. Being inferior to other predators, it is possible that diurnal hunting when most predators are inactive is an adaptation to avoid competition. Greater daytime activity, however, brings the cheetah into competition with vultures, who may also drive a cheetah away from a kill. However, this problem is minimized by the habit of dragging the kill into cover before eating.

The competitive disadvantage with large African carnivores is not confined to the feeding on its own kills. Large carnivores like lions, leopards and hyenas may actively seek cheetahs out and kill them. The alertness of cheetahs so frequently seen in the field is not only a sign of prey search, but also vigilance for the presence of enemies. In game reserves where there is an abundance of predators such as lions and spotted hyenas, the number of cheetah is low. The northern part of Namibia is a good example. In Etosha National Park, where large herds of springbok feed on the open plains, there is a surprising lack of cheetahs in the park. Although such an area provides ideal condi-

A cheetah cub flees from a wildebeest bull. Hunting is a learning process and cubs often misjudge their quarry.

Opposite:
An intent look on a male leopard's face follows the identification of a bicycle rider approaching along a nearby track. However, leopards are not inclined to attack people, unless they feel threatened.

A female leopard takes a nap in the seclusion of the bush.

Previous pages:
Although often seen in trees, leopards prefer the ground, particularly if they feel uncomfortable or threatened.

tions for cheetahs, it appears that the abundance of lions and possibly also hyenas is a major deterrent. There have been several attempts to re-introduce cheetahs to the park, without success, although ironically, cheetahs are common on farms bordering the park. In fact, farmers consider them pests because of the damage they cause to livestock, goats in particular. The local Department of Nature Conservation has endorsed a program to protect cheetahs on farmland by providing compensation to farmers who have lost livestock to cheetahs. The challenge of the program is to change the attitude of farmers towards cheetah and perhaps, to make use of their presence instead of regarding them as pests.

Of all large African predators, the cheetah is perhaps the least dangerous to man. Normally, cheetahs are timid in the presence of human observers on foot or in a vehicle. Unlike lions, for example, cheetahs will tend to avoid vehicles if they are parked on their path, and they will tend to take cover and hide in thick bush on the approach of a vehicle. In some parks, however, cheetahs that are accustomed to the presence of humans become very tame and even may use vehicles as their observation posts.

Much controversy surrounds the possible interference tourist vehicles cause to cheetahs. Being a diurnal

predator, tourists frequently have the opportunity to watch a cheetah stalking prey. In their eagerness to get close, onlookers pursue the cheetahs without considering that they disrupt the cheetahs' hunting. Although at times cheetahs may use vehicles for cover, by and large, the proximity of vehicles is extremely detrimental for cheetahs. Vehicle interference with animals is often cited as a dire consequence of ecotourism. Nonetheless, animals manage to adjust and alter their behavioral patterns to ease such pressures. Ultimately, it is the size of the reserve and consequently the availability of habitat combined with the pressures from outside the boundaries that determine the future success or failure of life cycles in the ecosystem.

Leopard

In many ways the leopard resembles the house cat, not only in its anatomical features, but also in its solitary and territorial habits. Its nocturnal movements and excellent camouflage make the leopard a particularly elusive creature, and a favorite attraction for tourists who visit the African bush.

Adults associate long enough to mate. Normally, males establish territories that overlap with several female home ranges. Females do not guard the home range zealously and maintain an enduring maternal bond until the offspring become self-sufficient, sometime before they reach the age of two years.

Since leopards are solitary animals, the development of body language and vocal communication is limited by comparison with lions and hyenas. The main vocalization is a rough rasping sound, like that of a saw being used on coarse wood. It is used to announce the presence of the territory's holder and to make contact between separated individuals. A females may also rasp to attract the attention of males when she is in heat, or to call her cubs. Males can assess the reproductive status of females by smelling her urine. Commonly, leopards leave distinctive scent stations on the boundaries of territories and home ranges. These grooves on the ground or sprays on bushes by the sides of prominent animal tracks and roads are information centers for leopards in the vicinity. In such a way, the solitary animal maintains contact with other leopards.

Leopards are opportunistic hunters, but will seldom revert to scavenging like hyenas. Typically, they hunt by means of an ambush, as leopards hardly ever run after prey. Similarly, leopards will never ambush prey from the branches of trees. They take advantage of darkness to find their prey, approaching slowly and patiently. They will wait for the prey to be distracted in order to gain a few meters. However, even at night, the success rate of hunting is relatively low. Although leopards have keen eyesight, it seems that their preferred prey – different gazelle or small-sized antelopes – also have acute senses.

On numerous occasions I followed leopards hunting. Typically, windy and stormy nights were more promising than quiet moonlit nights. I used to drive behind the leopard, using a spotlight only to shine where I was driving. I was careful not to disturb its intended prey, the nervous impala herds that moved restlessly knowing that danger was close by. As the leopard approached the impala herd, I would switch off the light. The impala would still be sensitive to the presence of the vehicle and tended to drift away. Nonetheless, natural sounds like the sudden wind gush and rustle of the grass, or a remote whooping sound of hyenas, were sufficient distraction for the leopard to edge a little closer. At the right moment, the leopard would dart from its cover. Like a flash, it would close the remaining distance and pounce on its prey, adjust its grip and reach for the throat.

Territory marking plays quite an important role in the life of an adult male. Here a leopard pauses after having urinated on a conspicuous bush along a road.

Leopards show remarkable agility of body and mind when opportunities arise. Unlike lions, that may stumble and get confused easily, leopards respond instantly to any change of conditions. If, for example, an impala herd comes rushing by, leopards seem to evaporate into thin air and emerge under the legs of the unsuspecting buck.

One night I was with some of the other staff and guests of the lodge in three open Landrovers, positioned some distance from a solitary grey duiker standing at the edge of a clearing. A leopard had been stalking the duiker for an hour, and was crouching in the grass a few meters away from it. Suddenly, an engine roared to life in the distance. This was the cue for the leopard and in three long leaps it reached the duiker. However, the buck was quick to respond and darted toward the thick cover of the bush. The leopard went after it. The duiker turned abruptly behind a stationary vehicle. In pursuit at full speed, it was too late for the leopard to change course. There was a hollow thud as the leopard crashed into the driver's door. To our surprise, the leopard scrambled underneath the vehicle and emerged on the opposite side. The duiker was equally surprised and hesitated for a moment. The leopard cut off the buck's escape route and, before the spotlights had caught up, the leopard had pounced on the duiker.

Being solitary and relatively small, the leopard is outranked by most African carnivores except for the cheetah. I witnessed dozens of encounters between leopards and hyenas, wild dog and lions. Although the leopard is well equipped to oppose its quarries and cause damage, it prefers to surrender its kill and disappear into the safety of the bush. Since the leopard is solitary, it cannot rely on a supply of food from group members if injury occurs. Adept tree climbers, leopards often drag their prey up trees, out of reach of scavengers, particularly hyenas. Although lions can climb trees, they are reluctant to do so if the tree trunk is high and does not provide good holding. Hyenas, with their acute senses and stamina, will often reach the site of the kill shortly after it had taken place. If the leopard is not quick enough to hoist its prey into a tree, a confrontation may ensue. One night I saw a juvenile leopard catching an impala. As it began feeding on the carcass, the crunching sound of the bones was fairly loud in the quietness of the bush and I expected some action. While I was fiddling with my camera flash, two hyenas rushed to the scene. It was too late for the leopard to take action, and in no time a bitter confrontation erupted. The two hyenas started chasing the leopard around the vehicle, while I was desperately trying to take a photograph. Eventually, the leopard scrambled to a tree and watched in frustration as his meal was devoured by the hyenas.

Although impala is a favorite prey for leopards, their acute senses and speed mean that they can be difficult to catch, and being an opportunistic predator, leopards will often opt for the most easily obtainable prey. In Savuti, for example, I got to know a female leopard that lived on chickens. Often guinea fowl roost in acacia trees, and my tent was built in the shade of acacia along the bank of the dry Savuti Channel. When I was alone in the camp, bush life would encroach and many nocturnal visitors would frequent the camp site. Among them was a female leopard which used to come to the camp along the access road from one of the rocky outcrops that characterize the Savuti area. Walking along the bank, the leopard used to flush guinea fowl from trees along its way. The guinea fowl would settle on the branches above my tent, but in the darkness they would struggle to find a place to settle and would crash into the branches while attempting to land. Gradually, the birds calmed down and their chirping ceased, at which point the leopard would make a move. Sometimes it would almost brush against the side of the tent where it was hidden from the birds. Any movement on my part around the tent, or even to the side of the bed, which would make the springs squeak, would spark off the hunt. The leopard would jump up the tree and reach the top branches in two leaps. Sometimes she caught two birds in one attempt. Plucking and feeding was done on the mattress at the entrance to the tent.

Leopards fear people, but are capable of killing them. The most likely reasons for a leopard to attack people are if it is cornered or if a female is defending her cubs. Since male leopards seldom exceed 60 kilograms in weight, they are even more reluctant than lions to confront man. Nonetheless, in general they are extremely unpredictable and hostile. When I was looking after animals in a zoo, I learnt that leopard cubs snarl and bite from a very early age, unlike lion cubs that are relatively tame. One day, while I was cleaning the access hall to the cages, a leopard bolted from the corner of its cage and grabbed my hand by pushing its paws through the bars. I managed to pull my hand free, but not before the leopard had left deep cuts that required hospital treatment. This was an introduction to the general attitude of leopards. Later on in Africa, I followed individual leopards closely almost on a daily basis. After a few months of observations, it was obvious that they recognized me. However, I never tried to make friends with them.

Opposite:
Blood trickles from the holes left by the leopard's canines on the impala's neck.

Lion

As part of the cat family, lions share the sleek and elegant appearance of most other members of the family. However, they differ in many respects. Living in social groups, or prides, makes them unique in the cat family. The size of a pride varies primarily according to the abundance, size and composition of prey species, but there may be as many as 40 lions in a pride. The pride is a matriarchal society over which males will fight for possession. Pride members are scattered in small groups or singly, although on a daily basis, individuals will come and go. Transient lions will sometimes attempt to invade and take over a pride of females, while other lions might pass through the territory and avoid contact with the resident pride. Hence, only continuous observations in a particular area will reveal the true composition of the pride.

Generally, the females of a pride are all related – descendants from females that have lived for generations in the same home range. Immigrant females may be accepted if the number of lionesses falls below the capacity of the pride to defend its territory and there are no offspring to fill the gap. Conversely, female cubs may have to emigrate when the pride reaches its capacity, determined by the size of prey and frequency of catch. An insufficient supply of meat will cause increased aggression among pride members that may lead to the departure of weaker juvenile females.

Males may monopolize the mating rights of several prides. The number of prides that males control may depend on the size of pride territories and the presence of competing lions. Male competition was perhaps a prominent factor in the evolutionary development of extensive sexual dimorphism. There is an obvious advantage in having a larger size and thicker mane in the competition for mating rights between males, although the ability to hunt is less marked in males than in females. Nonetheless, males are independent of the hunting skills of females, and may catch prey by themselves.

It takes a male five years to reach the size and weight of a mature lion. By the age of three, young males are evicted from a pride, because of the intolerance of the adult males. From then until maturation, when they take over the range of a pride, males live a nomadic life. They follow the migration of game and cross the territories of prides where they will be persecuted by the resident males if they are encountered.

One of the ways lions use to deter invaders and nomadic males is roaring. The roar of a lion is among the most prominent symbols of wild Africa, and in many nature reserves it is a frequent sound in the

A lioness gives birth to her cubs in a hidden place away from the pride. After the cubs reach the age of several weeks, the lioness will introduce them gradually to the pride.

night. The sound of a roar can be heard over several kilometers, although the bush dampens much of its intensity. My house in Sabi-Sabi was situated at the end of a row of staff houses. It bordered an old airstrip that was frequently used by the local lion pride. At one stage, two big and powerful males dominated the mating rights of the pride. To proclaim their rights, the males used to roar at night at the far side of the airstrip. Moonlit nights, when hunting ceased, were a favorite time. Whenever I heard them, I used to drive up to where they were in the open grass. Obligingly, the males would let me drive past and settle in between them. This became a ritual until one of the lions was killed. After this the lions turned and faced the vehicle, each male within a few meters. The side panels of the open vehicle intensified the roars, the panels resonating from the powerful blast of air. It was an overwhelming and yet enchanted encounter in the African night.

The strong social bonding among the members of a pride is the key to the lions' successful survival in the African bush. The function of the pride as a working team explains much of the inter- and intra-pride dynamics. The size of the team is an optimal solution that represents the conflicting factors of security in numbers and the desire for sexual dominance. A single territorial male can afford to defend his mating rights over a pride, if he is sufficiently aggressive and large enough to overpower intruders. Similarly, females may endure life-long associations, if their tendency to cooperate and avoid confrontation overrides their aggression. Nonetheless, wherever lions are plentiful, single males can rarely take over or keep a territory for long. Therefore, mating opportunities for transient males are limited to nomadic females who are more likely to lose their cubs.

In general, coalitions of males have a relatively brief reproductive career, seldom lasting more than two years. This is largely because the maintenance of weight and mane hair among lions does not last long after they reach the age of eight. As a result, large coalitions with males of different ages are more likely to hold for a longer period. A common practice among lions is to kill the cubs in a recently acquired pride. Older juveniles may escape with their lives but cannot survive unless their mothers leave with them. The lionesses may not remain indifferent to the killings and can defend their offspring vigorously, often at the risk of injury or death. But there is an evolutionary logic to this seemingly cruel behavior: lionesses normally produce cubs at intervals of two years and come into estrus when the cubs are about

Yet another early morning patrol in the bush, closely following a lion pride. The flattened ears indicate signs of irritation that they are being followed too closely.

Lions reach their prime at about five years of age.

Following pages:
A lion may extract the fluids it requires from its prey and subsist without drinking. But, if a water source is nearby, lions will drink, particularly after a large meal.

Lion cubs have no rights over a kill. The lioness is making this point clear to the cub.

one and a half years old, but the loss of a litter will cause the female to come into estrus and mate within a few weeks following the death of her cubs. Hence, males that are tolerant of cubs that they did not produce may miss the opportunity to breed, taking into consideration the fact that their tenure as pride leaders is approximately two years.

Evolution has also shaped the process of forming a new pride. Upon the arrival of new males, lionesses will accept the consequent infanticide as they might stand an even greater loss if the new lions fail to maintain the pride and other lions replace them. Thus, during a period that takes some four months, a newly formed pride engages in an unusual spurt of mating activity. Pregnant females may even go through apparent estrus, while other females may come into estrus but fail to ovulate. This period of infertility serves to protect the females against desertion by the new males, but it also helps to establish and reinforce bonds between the new males and the pride. During

this period, the females may mate with males from several coalitions. Thus, the period is an opportunity to examine the stability of coalitions and assess the prospects of their endurance.

While establishing a new pride, males will not fight over mating rights. The choice of mates is often a case of first-come, first-served. If, however, there is a clear distinction between the males, and one male appears in much better shape than the rest, the chances are that this male will control most mating rights. Unlike many herbivore species, there is no particular breeding season for lions, although a synchrony in breeding may be observed among pride members as it allows the females to share the burden of raising and protecting cubs.

The sight of lions mating is a common one in the African bush. The proximity of a male and a female is usually a reliable sign of a mating pair. The female may at first rebuff mounting attempts with snarls and slaps. Later, the female initiates mating by crouching and presenting before the lion. While mating, the female keeps rumbling and even growling, probably because she resents being straddled. A couple may copulate some 3000 times for every cub that survives to the yearling stage. The estrus period lasts approximately four days. During that period the couple may copulate at the rate of three times every hour for the entire period. The male may increase the rate of copulation, if two females are in estrus.

Shortly before giving birth, the lioness leaves the pride and her cubs are born in a well-hidden lair. After a month the mother may return to the pride with her cubs. Some lionesses, however, choose to raise their cubs by themselves – something which probably depends on the status of the lioness within the pride, as well as the nature of her character. A large and aggressive lioness, for example, may manage to care for her offspring by herself. When they join a pride, the cubs also appear at sites of kills. By their second month, the cubs are able to keep up with the pride. Weaning takes place around the eighth month.

Cub mortality is high and only about one cub in five reaches the juvenile stage. They are sometimes left alone for over a day while their mothers consort with other pride members, when they will stay closely hidden and, if disturbed, crawl into cramped areas for cover. They are also quick to take cover when adult lions are in the vicinity. The availability of food is an important factor in the survival rate of cubs, as the mother may abandon her cubs if food is scarce.

Moreover, the cubs may be killed by other predators such as hyenas, hence the advantage of several females raising cubs under the protection of the pride coalition. In Savuti, for example, a pride was studied and observed for more than a decade. Throughout this period, the six females of the prides produced offspring annually when they were fertile, yet none of the cubs survived. It was not clear what happened to the cubs, although the abundance of hyenas may have been the prime factor. Other factors included infanticide after a male pride take-over and, in one case, a mamba killed three cubs that were hidden underneath a bush.

The teamwork of a pride is perhaps best exemplified in hunting. Although lions can reach the speed of 50 to 60 kilometers per hour, most prey species of lions can reach a considerably higher speed. Accordingly, lions need to cooperate with other members of the pride. In addition, skill, patience, cunning and judgement determine their success rate. They have to get as close as possible to their designated prey, and then rely on the element of surprise and a burst of speed to chase the prey before it accelerates beyond the lions' reach. To get within effective range, lions rely primarily on stalking. An experienced lion will rarely charge unless it is within 30 meters of its quarry, but like many other carnivores, lions are highly opportunistic, and the intended victim is not always the one that lions pull down. Lions prefer to hunt at night when they can successfully use the cover of darkness to

A lioness scrambles to tighten her grip on a wildebeest cow she has just pulled down.

It is very difficult not to ascribe feelings to animals when observing intimate interactions like this lioness with her brother.

get closer to their prey. Daylight restricts lions to the ambush technique where they can remain motionless under the cover of bushes near a waterhole.

Watching lions stalking in the bush is a fascinating sight. The sensory organs are located towards the roof of the lion's skull, which means that lions can observe their prey without fully exposing the top of their head and disrupt the outlines of their cover. From their vantage point, lions scan the horizon for a suitable prey. Whenever I followed lions with a vehicle, which provided a better vantage point, the cats consistently picked up prey and dashed off in its direction before I knew what it was. This was usually during twilight and darkness hours, as lions see well in the dark. The eyes of a lions have extra-light-sensitive cell layers that reflect and translate the dim light of the bush into a composite picture of prey and cover. Lions also detect and respond to movement, with their strong reflexes allowing them to attempt a running approach towards an inattentive or distracted animal, freezing instantly and sinking to the ground when the quarry faces in their direction.

Most group hunts are conducted by the lionesses. Males usually trail behind and rush onto the scene of the kill when the prey is pulled down. The extraordinary coordination of lions during a hunt can look sophisticated on first sight. The lionesses spread out like a fan and stalk the prey with an expression of concentration on their faces. Some researchers have even suggested that the black stains on the back of the lionesses' ears allow them to communicate and coordinate during the hunt. While lions can achieve effective ambushes, it appears that lions completely ignore the direction of the wind, and they are often guilty of blatant mistakes that make their cooperative effort look rather silly. In fact, lions fail in approximately 80 percent of their attempts to catch prey. Visitors to game reserves who witness these attempts may also notice the moments after the chase. It is evident that a great amount of energy is used during a hunt. The expressions on lions' faces are not far from exhilaration after a successful hunt, or conversely, disappointment after a failure.

While antelopes have developed a number of techniques to divert lions, such as changing course abruptly or ranging in large herds, lions can lock onto their prey like a guided missile. As one who has survived a serious lion charge, it is obvious to me how lions avoid being distracted. During the chase, the eyes of the lion never leave its intended victim. While moving around bushes and across obstacles, their body turns, twists, and swirls, but the eyes stay on the same level above the ground, never leaving the prey. Once within striking distance of its prey, a lion has to overpower and kill it without getting injured in the process. Game the size of impala is brought down with a slap on the hindquarters, or by tipping it over or clutching it with the front paws. The prey is then quickly killed with a bite to the neck or the throat.

As the size of the prey increases, so the risk of injury becomes higher. Buffaloes are relatively slow and their movements in the bush are noisy, so lions can approach closely without much effort if the wind direction is in their favor. A successful kill of a buffalo weighing half a ton can sustain a pride of ten lions for several days. Yet, buffaloes are aggressive creatures and can cause a lot of harm. They may not be deterred by lions approaching and may counter-charge and stampede the lions. Consequently, lions either seek isolated members of the herd or try to isolate calves. Old buffaloes are normally avoided, simply because their sheer power and weight can break the bones of several lions before it is pulled down.

Lions may also kill young elephants, if they are found unprotected. This normally happens in the vicinity of waterholes, if an elephant becomes disorientated and looses contact with its parent group. This is a golden opportunity for lion prides. Within minutes, the elephant is overpowered, its family too far away and oblivious of the drama. In Savuti, a pride of lions was known to specialize on young elephants, taking calves and yearlings up to four years of age.

Play amongst lion cubs is an important part of learning hunting techniques. Cubs spend a great amount of time stalking each other, sprinting and grabbing one another much as adults do with their prey. Play is also important in enhancing cohesion among members of the pride and a subtle way of establishing a pecking order. Since many of the female cubs have a good chance of staying with the same pride, they assess through playing at an early stage the individual characteristics of each lioness. Males, on the other hand, rarely join in play sessions after they reach the age of three. Nonetheless, to maintain cohesion among coalition members, these males rub heads against each other whenever they meet. The intensity of this greeting ceremony may serve as an indication of the relationship between different males in a group.

Lions respond aggressively to people. No matter how cuddly lions may appear in the bush, they remain dangerous and highly unpredictable. Although they are social creatures, the body language of the lion is subtle and not exemplary like that of the elephant. Nonetheless, in nature reserves lions do become tolerant to the presence of vehicles, and may come and lie down in the shade created by a vehicle. In private game reserves where night drives are conducted, hunting lions can be viewed from open vehicles. The lions will ignore the presence of people in the vehicle, despite the fact that they are fully exposed, although if a person stands, normally to get a better view, lions will respond. It seems that if people are seated in the open vehicles, lions perceive them as part of it. If,

I became so familiar with the habits of the local lion pride at Sabi-Sabi that I was able to anticipate with considerable accuracy the chance of a successful hunt taking place and the location where the prey would be ultimately pulled down. Here, the pride had just caught an impala.

however, someone stands up, they disrupt the shape of the vehicle and the lion identifies a human being, which it fears and resents.

The incidence of lions attacking humans is rare. If they are encountered on foot, lions rather prefer to avoid people and retreat to the safety of the bush. If surprised, however, lions will respond by attacking, principally because they feel threatened. Thus the best way to avoid being eaten by lions is to make yourself obvious while walking in the bush. In particular this rule applies to the tourist camps throughout northern Botswana which are not surrounded by fences. Lions start prowling at dusk, and are fully active by night time and may even wander through a camp site. Visitors should also close their tents, as lions are curious creatures and will investigate everything in their territory. An open fly sheet is an invitation for lions to step into the tent, and most cases of tourists losing their lives to lions has been as a result of tents being left open after dark, or of people sleeping on the ground in the open. Although a tent is no match to the claws of lions, a closed tent poses a psychological obstacle. Knowing this, it is always a nice feeling to wake up in the morning in a tent in the heart of the African bush, to step outside and stretch, and notice spoor on the sandy ground indicating that a pride of lions walked past while you were asleep.

Fieldwork often requires the researcher to walk in the field to gather data. During one of the early field excursions I made in Sabi-Sabi, I set out to explore the banks of a major river course. The terrain was difficult to negotiate with a vehicle, and I was happy to take the opportunity of a long walk in the bush. The atmosphere was serene, with riverine birds singing in the shade of the dry river course. Earlier that morning, I had driven out to the resident lion pride. At that time, I recognized prides by counting (as opposed to individual recognition), and all ten members were there. The truth was that I did not know the actual composition of the pride, and a female was missing, but I did not pay much attention. Having seen the composition of riverine vegetation along the dry riverbed, I started heading back to camp. I chose to walk on the bank and examine the transition of bush to the riverine forest. At one stage, I came into a natural clearing that looked like a small meadow. I heard a deep sound. Innocently, I thought it strange that a Landrover was negotiating its way through this rocky terrain. Then I heard a second and louder growl. If I had not been in this situation, it could have been very comical. Once I realized that I was actually hearing the growl of a lion, I started to search for the source of the sound.

Some 40 meters in front of me in the open grass were three tiny cubs playing, with their mother crouching low next to them, ready to pounce. I froze. Running away was out of the question, that I knew, but I was armed only with a pair of binoculars. The lioness made her move, darting towards me, running with a high gait in the way I had seen lions charge hyenas or other lions, to make herself as large as she could. Her big emerald eyes locked on me. I took a step forward and yelled at her. Stunned, the lioness stopped and crouched. The growling intensified. I thought my best idea was to increase the distance between us in the hope that the lioness would loose interest. I took a step backwards. It worked. The lioness remained motionless. I took another step. Slowly, I started retreating, never taking my eyes off her. Then I thought that ignoring the lioness altogether would help. I turned and started walking away casually. This was a mistake – when I turned my gaze sideways to confirm that the lioness was still where I had left her, I saw her looming shadow dashing towards me. I turned and yelled, making a sudden movement towards her. The lioness stopped on her heels a few yards away and crouched.

I was determined not to give away my precious binoculars. Instead, I picked up a rock, never letting my eyes leave the lioness. I began to feel the adrenaline surge vanishing and reality set in. I was stuck with an angry lioness protecting her cubs with no way out and no weapon to protect myself. After a period that seemed like eternity, I decided to revert to the initial strategy, and attempted to increase the distance between us. I resumed the backward walk. This time the lioness did not budge. Encouraged, I carried on walking backward, careful not to trip and fall, or take my eyes off her. I reached the bank of the dry river. The lioness sat on her hindquarters to have a better view of me. I disappeared down the riverbed and started running up the opposite bank. Fortunately, she did not follow me.

In retrospect, it seems that I was very lucky. I remembered not to take my eyes off the lion. Looks distract them from their initial intention. The backside of an adversary is an invitation to take the spoils of victory. The lioness was highly motivated, as she felt that her cubs were threatened. An injured lion is the only other situation where lions will charge in an attempt to kill. This time, it seems that my position in relation to the cubs worked in my favor. As I retreated, the distance between the cubs and me increased. Although the lioness was close to me and ready to pounce, she felt less motivated to do so because the cubs were no longer endangered.

Warthog

Although relatively small in size, the warthog is a conspicuous resident of African nature reserves. Attitudes towards warthogs among visitors vary from affection to antipathy, yet compassion takes over if they encounter a predator killing a warthog. It is not certain that the distinctive erection of its tail is really an alarm signal for other warthog. Nonetheless, the sight of a warthog trotting at full speed is amusing. Warthogs are slower than most savanna antelopes, and accordingly they will head for the nearest burrow and dive head-first inside. Adults then turn around and present the predator with their formidable tusks. Depending on the size and number of predators, warthogs may turn around and fight their attacker. On a number of occasions I witnessed warthogs chase a leopard that had attempted to take a yearling or a piglet.

Warthogs are the only kind of pig adapted to the conditions of the savanna. The warthog grazes on short grass and reverts to digging and eating rhizomes and bulbs when the grass is too dry during the dry season. It adopts a unique posture while grazing, walking on its calloused wrists. They are generally observed in groups – their basic social unit being known as a sounder, which consists of females and their young. The social organization is based on a matriarchal structure where females maintain stable bonds with offspring that may continue throughout successive breeding cycles. Males become solitary or associate in sub-adult groups upon maturation.

Burrows are an inseparable part of warthog life. With their strong snout, warthogs can easily dig and expand burrows initiated by an aardvark in the base of termite mounds. Although sounders seldom meet or exchange members, they use the same network of burrows on a first-come, first-served basis. They use burrows on a rotating basis and may keep as many as ten holes in one period.

Right:
The bond between mother and infant is strong in the matriarchal warthog society. Here, a mother grooms her grown piglet.

Yearling warthogs associate in small groups that are the descendants of the original sounder. The erection of hairs at the top of the mane is an indication of excitement.

The warts of the male warthog are skin appendages that may serve as protection during confrontations with other males.

Opposite:
A recognizable feature of warthogs is their raised tail during retreat and escape from predators. The trait is so imbedded that warthogs will keep their tail raised even when running at full speed.

The bushbuck is a shy antelope that favors riverine areas with lush vegetation.

Bushbuck

A shy, yet common and widely distributed antelope, the bushbuck is essentially an ecotone species, preferring to forage at the edges of forests and dense woodlands. Nonetheless, unlike the impala, the bushbuck prefers the sanctuary of the bush and ventures out to the open only in search of edible plants, encouraged by the presence of other bushbucks and animals that share common predators. However, the bushbuck is predominantly a browser, eating leaves of shrubs and forbs, and it will only occasionally revert to grazing tender new grass. Invariably, they are found in riverine areas near water where a wide diversity of plant species satisfies their nutritional requirements and provides sufficient cover.

The bushbuck is a solitary antelope, and the most common associations are that of mothers and their calves. Nonetheless, they do not avoid each other actively and their home ranges overlap. Calves are dropped in dense cover and do not accompany the mother into the open until they are four months old. The maternal bond is strong, and thus the mother and calf are typically engaged in mutual licking of the body parts beyond the other's reach.

The bushbuck relies a good deal on its pattern of coat for camouflage and will remain motionless upon the approach of a predator. If detected and pursued, however, the bushbuck dashes for cover while raising its white-edged tail. Injured bushbuck are known to be highly aggressive animals which will not hesitate to attack and they are quite able to kill people.

Impala

This medium-sized antelope is a common sight in many southern African savanna ecosystems. It reaches high densities wherever it finds food, and visitors to game reserves quickly become accustomed to the sight of impala and, as a consequence, often ignore this handsome creature. In fact, the impala is very different to other antelopes, to the extent that it is classified as a separate tribe. They are mostly found in ecotone areas, meaning that they favor the transition zones between woodlands and open grasslands. Due to its specific ecological requirements and dependence on surface water, impala will either be found in very high aggregations, or not at all.

The impala prefers to graze if green grass is available. During the dry season, when grass nutrients are absorbed and concentrated in the roots, impala switch to browse on the foliage of trees and forbs. The ability to alternate between different kinds of forage enables it to live a sedentary life and remain in one area all year round. It can also thrive in areas that have been damaged as a result of over-grazing and the encroachment of bush, where the natural vegetation has given way to plants associated with disturbed areas.

Although males live a solitary life, bachelor groups are found in the vicinity of – or mingled with – female herds. In southern Africa, however, where seasons are distinguished, males establish territories for a short period of time during the rut. They mark the territories by rubbing the glandular secretion from their forehead on bushes and by defecating in middens throughout the territory. Females live in discrete herds within traditional home ranges. The turnover rate in the female herd is very low. Most males, however, leave their natal herd by the age of four and move far enough to be placed within the range of different female herds, thus avoiding inbreeding. The female herd is essentially a homogeneous unit where family and peer group connections are non-existent. There is no sign of a pecking order and females normally do not maintain body contact, except for reciprocal grooming. Nonetheless, the activities of the herd are closely synchronized – probably as a kind of anti-predator mechanism.

Vigorous territorial displays are seen only in the southern African male impala, and then only for a few months. The size of a territory depends on the quality of habitat, the availability of resources within it and local impala population densities. In principal, the more available the resources and the higher the densities of impalas, the smaller the territories will be. Impala males tend to establish their territories annually – close to the location of the territory of the previous year. Males invest a considerable amount of time rounding up and attending all females that enter their territories. A male will advertise the possession of a territory by different means depending on its vigor and opportunities, but the roaring of adult male impalas is a common sound during the months of April and May in southern Africa. In addition, males proclaim the boundaries of the territories by scent marking from a gland situated on the forehead. Impala males and females also have metatarsal glands that probably serve general purposes, such as the maintenance of contact between individuals in the thick bush.

Since impalas are abundant wherever they are found, they constitute a large proportion of the diets

Following pages:
Impala can extract moisture from their food, but if the opportunity to drink surface water arises, they will not hesitate to take it.

The agility and speed of the impala enables it to escape and outrun most of the large predators of the bush.

The nyala is almost entirely confined to the Lowveld in southern Africa and can be found in low-lying and densely wooded habitats.

of large predators. Unlike antelopes that favor open grasslands, such as wildebeest, the impala is more vulnerable to ambush from within the thick bush. Nonetheless, with their alertness and acute senses, impalas are quick to take flight and pose a difficult quarry for any predator. Through observing the behavior of impala herds, it is possible to locate the position of a leopard. A suspicious impala will abruptly stop walking and freeze while its ears will rotate to pick up the slightest sound. If it fails to see the source of disturbance, the impala will move its head to see more. The impala may resume grazing and suddenly lift its head and look again in the same direction. This trick may deceive a lion or a leopard stalking the herd. Other members of the herd may follow if one impala insists on looking in one particular direction. Finally, if the predator is detected, an alarm bark follows. The closer the predator and the more imminent the danger, the larger the number of individual alarm calls.

If a predator charges, the impala runs for safety, jumping high and trying to distract the attention of a predator by changing its course abruptly. If all fails, then the rules of probability determine that individuals that stay in larger herds are less likely to be caught. However, as territorial males are reluctant to leave their territory, they are likely to run in a circle, coming back to the point where they were flushed initially. Large predators also know this.

Nyala

This handsome antelope is almost entirely confined to the Lowveld of southern Africa, particularly low-lying and densely wooded habitats near water. It is a mixed feeder, browsing on leaves and pods or grazing, especially during the wet season when the grass is nutritious and has proportionally lower fiber contents. The nyala's basic social organization consists of an adult female with both her latest offspring and those from the year before. Female associations may be formed, but they are of short duration and occur only if females have young. Males do not actively avoid one another and groups of males may be formed and remain stable, if they belong to the same peer group. However, as males mature, their tendency is to remain solitary. Males check the reproductive status of females whenever they encounter them, but do not remain in the vicinity if none of the females is in estrus. Aggression in males is displayed through digging and tossing soil with their horns, and bulls will erect the hairs on their rump during an encounter, but generally interactions between males are peaceful, even if an estrus female is close by.

A six-year-old kudu bull browses. The length of the horns and number of curls indicate its age.

Right:
This kudu calf was born a few hours before I found this scene. Knowing that at this early stage, the calf might confuse me for its mother, I took the photograph and retreated hastily.

Following pages:
Kudus are high jumpers and a sturdy fence taller than 2.5 meters is required to keep them within a designated area.

Greater kudu

This gracious antelope is a true bush resident which favors thickets, subsisting also in settled areas as long as enough cover is available. The kudu is a popular game animal in South African private nature reserves, but being a high jumper, managers of reserves have to erect sturdy fences that are at least two and a half meters in height. The kudu feeds almost exclusively on browse that includes the leaves of trees and shrubs, forbs and fallen fruits and leaves.

Kudus are found in groups and are not territorial. Core herds include females and their offspring, and although mergers of herds are common, they do not last long. Males associate in bachelor groups that include mature males, but it is not clear whether there is an established hierarchy among the members of the herd. Contests between two bulls over the possession of mating rights are rare.

The bark of a kudu is a good indication that a large predator is nearby. Unlike impalas, kudus will remain silent until they ascertain the extent of the danger. In fact, the common anti-predator strategy for the kudu is to stand in silence. With their superb camouflage and preferred habitat types, kudus blend well into the background of the bush and will let an observer walk very close to them before taking flight. Alternatively, kudus may retreat into the safety of the bush long before their presence has been detected. When fleeing, their tail is raised and displays a white band. The function of the band is not clear since it is obvious to the predator and not to other kudus that run in different directions.

Blue wildebeest

A common resident of East and southern African savannas, the wildebeest does not elicit much enthusiasm from visitors. Nonetheless, they contribute much to the total biomass of open savanna residents and they are an important component of these ecosystems. It is a grazer with a broad muzzle and wide incisors adapted to bulk feeding on short grass. In East Africa, wildebeest are found in large aggregations, whereas in southern Africa their local densities are much smaller.

The social organization of wildebeest depends on the nomadic nature of different populations. Their movements are determined by the availability and distribution of green pastures and the proximity of water sources. Resident populations tend to be sedentary and dispersed. A territorial bull will remain on its own, while cows stay in herds of about ten animals. The composition of the cow herds is quite stable and transient females are normally excluded both by the females and the dominant male. In large aggregations, however, the transition of females from one group to another is common.

At the age of one, juveniles join herds comprised of their peers. Bachelor herds are found attached to these groups, but tend to keep a greater distance from bulls than the female herds will. They stay in marginal areas for grazing where they are the least harassed by territorial bulls. In large concentrations, they mingle with females as territorial bulls cannot distinguish them from the rest. Territorial bulls maintain small territories and are relatively tolerant to the close proximity of other territorial bulls. In sedentary populations, the territories are held year round although most of the mating is done during a three-week rut period from mid-March to the beginning of April. However, only about half of all adult male wildebeest hold territories at any given time.

Wildebeest display aggression in several ways. Nodding the head is a common sign of impatience and may be performed by males and females alike. Interestingly, wildebeest do not have appeasing or submissive postures. Unlike the zebra, for example, wildebeest do not share a diverse range of communication cues and neither are they interactive, such as in play. Fighting, however, is common, particularly in the rut season at the peak of territorial activity. Rutting bulls with females do not engage rivals in ritual fights, but simply run at and ram invaders.

The timing of calving and rut season are synchronized with the changes of the seasons to ensure that the birth of calves coincides with optimal conditions for growth. Given an eight-month gestation period,

Opposite:
A time of plenty. A wildebeest bull takes a mouthful of nutritious grass species (*Panicum maximum*).

This unusual scene shows a yearling wildebeest attempting to suckle from its mother. By the end of the first year, the mother gives birth to another calf and disassociates from her previous offspring.

A solitary wildebeest attending its territory.

wildebeest have a finely tuned reproductive cycle. Few calves born ahead of the three-week calving season survive if large predators, such as lions and hyenas, are abundant in the area. However, if early-born calves survive their first two months, after which the coloration of their coats changes to something similar to that of the adults, they have an advantage over those born later. Calves are born in the midst of a herd, with the cows normally grouped at that time according to their reproductive status. Labor lasts a little over an hour, and within five minutes of its birth, the calf is on its feet seeking the udder. In its first two days, a calf learns to coordinate its movements and, more importantly, becomes imprinted on its mother. This innate behavior helps the newborn to find and stay close to its mother at all times. It is particularly important during the early stages of life when the threats are numerous and frequent. The imprinting process starts when the cow licks the calf immediately after birth, and then with the first successful suckling. The mother then recognizes her calf by its scent and rejects all other calves. However, this does mean that lost calves are doomed to starvation or predation.

Giraffe

A classic example of the theory of evolution demonstrating successful ecological adaptation, the giraffe has access to foliage well beyond the reach of all other large herbivores apart from the elephant. Large giraffe bulls can reach up to feed on the crowns of trees six meters high, and as bulls are about one meter taller than cows, it is possible to distinguish between the sexes simply by observing the height at which different animals are browsing. Another quite prominent difference between the sexes is the shape of the horns. Male horn growth involves a unique process whereby the bone of skin origin is deposited over the surface of the skull, except where the muscles join. At later stages of growth, the bone accumulates as knobs at the base of the skull, over the eyes and on the nose. The horns differ in that females have slender shapes with tufts of hair at the top, whereas mature males have blunt protrusions.

Giraffes have profound effects on the shapes of trees, with pyramid-shaped trees the result of intensive giraffe browsing. Giraffes may suppress the growth of trees by pruning young trees and keeping them at lower heights for years. Its narrow muzzle, long tongue and flexible upper lip enable the giraffe to strip leaves from branches or select individual leaves between sharp thorns. The tongue is protected from thorns by rows of sturdy papillae. Giraffes require to

Opposite:
A giraffe calf takes its first steps several minutes after birth.

Giraffe bull browses. The horns of the giraffe bull are appendages of bone growth that cover the complete top part of the skull.

drink once every three days depending on the availability of green leaves or dew on the leaves.

Giraffes form loose associations of individuals with more or less similar ages. The cohesion within the group is rather small and giraffes cluster together when browsing on the same tree or upon the sight of a predator. There is no leader to the group and the movements of the group are uncoordinated, with individuals continually leaving or joining. Nonetheless, with their high vantage point, giraffes can maintain visual contact with other individuals in the vicinity. The most lasting bond in the giraffe society is between mothers and their calves. Calves tend to be found in the same group, which forces the mothers to remain in the same locality. Some form of hierarchy exists among females, as it can be observed that some individuals may give way upon the approach of another.

Males associate in bachelor groups. By three years of age, when males reach puberty, they leave their natal group and wander out of the home range of the group. Males tend to be solitary as they mature and, other than feeding, spend much of their time assessing the reproductive status of females in different groups. Consequently, males are mostly seen in the company of females and their young, but the composition of the group is likely to alter from one day to the next.

Males assert dominance over their peers. The position of a male in the hierarchy is commonly a function of seniority and is also decided through confrontations and contests between sub-adults in the

Opposite:
While a female giraffe attends her grown calf, a male investigates her reproductive status by smelling her urine.

A giraffe stands on the ecotone, the edge of the transition between two habitat types, in this case a woodland and an open savanna grassland.

bachelor herds. Males may assess the power of a rival by leaning heavily against one another. The winner of a ritualized confrontation can be predicted by assessing the postures of the contestants and noting the one that stands most erect. The movements of the necks appear rhythmical and synchronized, but are the result of mutual efforts to administer and brace against blows. As a result, blows seldom land solidly, but the impact of the blows is considerable and there are clear advantages to age, weight and height.

The giraffe has few enemies because of its superior size. In addition, good vision and speed make giraffes untouchables. Lions may pull down adult giraffes if they manage to avoid their powerful hooves, which can deliver a lethal blow. In the Kruger National Park, lions have devised a method to trip giraffes by taking advantage of the tarred roads and driving giraffes in the direction of the roads in the hope that they will slip on the tarmac. In the Sabi-Sand, lions trip giraffes by causing confusion during night hunts. Once, a fully grown giraffe fell on a Landrover during a chase. The lions were equally confused and the giraffe quickly recovered and dashed off to safety. Unfortunately, the tracker sitting on the front part of the vehicle sustained internal injuries and later died at the hospital.

Small giraffe calves are particularly vulnerable to predation by lions and spotted hyenas. The vigilance of mothers is the best protection the calves have. Mothers may choose open plains which afford better visibility. They conceal the calves in clumps of bushes and browse some distance away from the calf, ever on the alert. The mothers may actively defend the calf using her hooves, although this is done as a last resort. The best chance of survival for a calf lies in speedy growth so that it can outrun a lion. Thus, the more time the calf spends resting, so the chances that food intake will be utilized for growth are greater.

Buffalo

The buffalo is placed among Africa's "Big Five" with good reason. With its formidable body and notorious aggression and cunning, particularly when injured, the buffalo acquired a reputation as a preferred trophy animal among old-time hunters. Nowadays, the sight of large herds in the open savanna raising clouds of dust is a reminder of the way Africa used to be.

The buffalo is the largest of the African bovids and reaches high densities in swamps and flood plains as well as in mountain grasslands and forests with a rich grass undergrowth. Like their relative, the domestic cow, the buffalo is a bulk grazer that subsists on tall and coarse grass. Browsing on forbs and shrubs also

takes place, particularly during the height of the dry season in southern Africa. However, the proportion of browse in the annual diet is low and is merely intended to supplement their dietary needs at times when grasses are dry and have poor nutritional value. In its preference for tall pastures, the buffalo also plays a pioneering role in the succession of grazing, by reducing grasslands to the height preferred by more selective feeders such as wildebeest and zebra.

The buffalo is a highly gregarious and nomadic animal that forms societies dominated by males, although they are not territorial. Buffaloes are distributed in discrete population units that remain in separate and traditional home ranges. The quality of habitats and local conditions determine the size of

Buffalo calves are vulnerable to large predators and will seek the safety of the herd for protection.

herds, with open grasslands with high grass productivity supporting larger herds. The population units do not intermingle. Transient animals that attempt to join either of the units are subjected to continuous harassment and are kept on the periphery. Sedentary old bulls remain in separate herds throughout the year. Bachelor herds, prime bulls and sub-adults separate from the main breeding herd during the dry season when no breeding takes place. Females and young may also move away to smaller units during the dry season when preferred long grass pastures are reduced to isolated patches close to water sources.

Related cows form the basic units of the buffalo society. There is no hierarchy among the adult cows, but a hierarchy of dominance is established among the bulls during the breeding season. Bulls and sub-adult males that join such a herd acquire a rank according to age and size. Females stay in their natal group as they mature. The maternal bond with males, by contrast, ends with adolescence after which males associate in bachelor sub-groups. Juvenile and sub-adult males tend to stay away from bulls.

Efficient communication among the members of a herd is critical because large herds require a high degree of coordination in darkness. It can be assumed that the olfactory sense is well developed in the buffalo to detect predators and for individual recognition. Vocal communication is also well developed, although by comparison to the domestic cow, the frequency of calls is lower. Nonetheless, scientists were able to distinguish between calls that serve as a signal to move, move in a specific direction, to announce the proximity of a water source, to identify a herd and position, an alarm call, aggression towards other members of the herd, a mother-to-calf call, a calf's distress call and a brief bellow that signals that all is well while grazing.

Fights between bulls are violent, but usually brief. The two bulls charge from a distance and ram each other only once. The impact is borne on the bosses of the horns, which are much more developed in bulls than in cows. The loser turns away and runs. Sparring, in contrast, is a common exercise that serves as a form of play as well as for sub-adults to assert dominance. The contact between the bulls when they spar is longer and involves milder force.

Bulls regularly monitor female reproductive status by urine testing and can prompt the female to urinate by licking the vulva. They then lift their upper lips in a posture that exposes olfactory cells on the palate, grouped on the vomeronasal organ. This behavior is typical to most ungulate species and known by the German word "Flehmen."

In the world of the buffalo, the olfactory sense is dominant. Here, a buffalo bull smells the urine of a cow to assess her reproductive status. The buffalo grimaces, thus exposing the vomeronasal organ situated on top of the palate.

Buffaloes respond to the appearance of large predators and man by fleeing. However, a mobbing response can also occur in response to a distress call by a calf. When this happens, the buffaloes will approach the source of the disturbance in a line abreast and perform alarm postures in which they raise their heads and hiss. Buffaloes close ranks when they are attacked by lions, their major predator, in order to make it difficult for the lions to single out an individual.

Fire

In semi-arid savannas throughout the world, fire is recognized as quite an important ecological factor in developing and maintaining productive and stable grass communities. In the past, before settlements and agricultural practices became as commonplace as today, fire was initiated by lightning during thunderstorms. In southern Africa, heavy thunderstorms occur during the rainy season. Early in the spring, with the onset of the first rains, the grass is still dry and is quite easily ignited by lightning.

Pastoral humans had considerable influence on grasslands by changing the frequency and intensity of natural fire regimes. However, most of the changes brought about by the new fire regimes were detrimental to the natural vegetation, as frequent fires cause the decline of the vegetation biomass of both trees and grasses. In principle, the vegetation structure of semi-arid savannas evolved under the influence of fire. As such, many grass and tree species are considered to be immune, at least partially, to the effects of intensive heat. Grasses absorb the nutrients from leaves during the dry winter and only fibrous leaves burn, thus enhancing the potential of new grass growth. The bark of many trees is sufficiently thick to protect the core and thus the sensitive growing tissues from the heat of a fire. As I have witnessed often enough many savanna trees are able to escape the detrimental effects of fire once they reach the height of three meters.

The detrimental effect of human settlement on fire patterns meant that when nature reserves came to be demarcated, the issue of a burning policy as a tool in the management of natural vegetation for the maintenance of natural cycles became a source of dispute because of the lack of data. The dynamics of fire and its influence on the environment are complex. Fire has composite effects on soils, land surface, water, vegetation and animals. Its effects are highly unpredictable, and thus managers of game reserves are reluctant to deploy fire as a means of achieving their objectives, such as combating bush encroachment, enhancing grass productivity and increasing vegetation diversity.

Fire is a natural phenomenon in the savanna ecosystem. Most plants are not affected by the fire and replace burnt parts with new shoots shortly after the fire has occurred.

Habitat management

Bush encroachment and erosion are two types of habitat degradation frequently encountered in semi-arid savannas. Habitat degradation can culminate in an irreversible decline in species diversity and reduction in the resilience of an ecosystem. In other words, a savanna woodland habitat may become a desert instead of regenerating to its former condition. Bush encroachment entails the invasion of previously open grassland by shrub and scrub forms of woody plants, and bush clearance and/or burning are considered to be important aspects in the management and rehabilitation of semi-arid savannas. Unfortunately, little is known about the causes behind the encroachment of bush and the dynamics of habitat degradation, especially in areas where the extent and patterns of human intervention are difficult to assess.

In recent years, managers in the Sabi-Sand became extremely concerned with bush encroachment and habitat degradation in the reserve. Aerial photographs showed that in the past 40 years, encroachment has occurred in some parts of the reserve, while degradation was quite evident from the loss of basal cover and increased gully and sheet erosion. Preliminary observations suggested that the depletion of soil moisture in upper soil levels and over-grazing by game and livestock in former cattle ranches induced the invasion of bush.

I began my Ph.D. and my association with Sabi-Sabi on the premise that I would look into the reasons behind the encroachment of bush in the reserve as part of my thesis and, as a result, formulate guidelines for the future conservation of the area. By the time that I started the fieldwork, nearly 20 percent of the reserve area had been bush-cleared and erosion was quite substantially controlled within certain areas by slowing surface water runoff. I monitored some of the rehabilitated areas that were characterized by an increase in grass cover, along with adjacent bush-encroached areas, to gather information about the underlying reasons for encroachment. In addition, I compared the frequency of visits of ungulates such as zebra, wildebeest, kudu and impala in clearings and encroached areas.

Beyond gathering information on the status of the reserve and the success of habitat development, I felt that I should provide the managers with a tool to assess the effectiveness of different treatments. After I completed my research, I still wanted to advise managers on appropriate steps for effective habitat management. There was already a tool available for such a purpose, called a computer expert system. A key cap-

A man-made grassland. Habitat reclamation work can take different forms, but some mechanical forms may be detrimental and defy the original objective to conserve the habitats.

Intensive fires may bring about the demise of trees. Controversy often surrounds questions about the frequency of burning, as plants may have a limited ability to recover from the aftermath of a fire.

Following pages:
Impala forage in an area that suffered from heavy erosion. Following some habitat work, grasses and forbs began to sprout and partially restore the ground cover, thus halting further erosion.

The methodology I used during the course of fieldwork included observations on the feeding patterns of wildebeest.

Opposite:
At the beginning of the rainy season, it was a mistake to open the window at night for fresh air, as winged termites would swarm into the room.

ability of an expert system is its ability to incorporate qualitative data in decision-making. In other words, the user can have a sort of dialog with the computer, which can answer questions or say, for example, "I do not know". Furthermore, the system can overcome the lack of scientific information and still make a viable suggestion for managers to pursue. In this particular case, the expert system extracted the relevant ecological information that applied to strategies of habitat rehabilitation. Thus, I designed the expert system to assist local managers of game reserves to decide how to conduct bush clearance, erosion control and burning to meet their objectives.

In order to reclaim habitats, one first has to identify degraded habitats that require treatment. The geomorphology, soil features and the extent of sheet and gully erosion were used to effectively evaluate the extent of degradation which was expressed in qualitative terms (the program uses the terms "none," "light," "moderate" and "severe"). All habitat parameters were then evaluated in relation to the objectives of the managers, as well as the prevailing conditions in terms of the current season and rainfall patterns. For example, when you are considering the viability of the maintenance of medium to tall grass areas, if the previous rainy season was relatively dry and the past five years

were also dry, then it would be less viable to maintain the grassland through burning.

When the program was operated on a personal computer, it searched for indications of degradation in the selected area, such as erosion, soil capping and bare areas. It was not compulsory, however, for the program to resolve a decision in favor of rehabilitation if evidence for degradation was found. Rather, the state of degradation, manifested through the extent of topsoil runoff, basal ground cover and degree of slope, would indicate the urgency in treating the area. Moreover, the user could have objectives that required the presence of "degraded" conditions, such as for the maintenance of a high density of impala that prefer over-grazed areas. An abundance of impala would, in turn, attract their predators, leopard and lion, considered to be major tourist attractions. In such cases, a compromise could be achieved by recommending the minimal steps required to prevent an acceleration of degradation in the area. This involved sealing eroded drainage lines and packing sheet-eroded areas without performing bush clearance. These procedures would slow down water runoff, and gradually halt the disappearance of topsoil.

When I constructed the expert system, it was important to stay in touch with the layman's environ-

ment and avoid making it another academic exercise. Hence, the program was designed to associate the relevant ecological information with the professional profiles and requirements of individual users. User types were identified according to their commitment to the area, their capability to utilize the natural resources on a sustainable yield basis, and their need for short-term revenues. The commitment of the manager or the owner was assessed in terms of the length of time that users would like to spend in the reserve. Similarly, the potential of the area for natural resource utilization was evaluated in relation to the capital the program users were willing to invest.

In the following examples, two different users are considered. User 1 was characterized as an owner of a private reserve that did not require a substantial utilization of the available natural resources, had no need for fast revenues, and had only little capital to invest in habitat work. User 2 was leasing an area in a nature reserve. He wished to maximize the revenues from natural resources on a short-term basis and had some capital for habitat work. Both users considered the same area and utilized the same pool of ecological database. A preliminary habitat assessment was performed by verifying the degree of slope, rockiness, clay composition, the abundance of gully and sheet erosion, soil capping, extent of basal cover and composition, and density of bush and scrub. There were some signs of degradation in terms of gully erosion and moderate bush encroachment. Habitat assessment incorporated topography, soils, vegetation features and extent of degradation. However, additional ecological criteria differed according to the requirements of individual users. For the first user a burning regime to combat bush encroachment by utilizing the existing fuel load was considered because the emphasis was on low-cost management over a long period of time. The program also recommended that gully erosion be stopped immediately to prevent further habitat degradation. For the second user, the advantages of accommodating higher densities of a variety of large herbivore species for game viewing and as a meat source were weighed against the high costs of bush clearance. Essentially, an abundance of any particular herbivore species would depend on the existing habitat features and the expected outcome of habitat manipulation by humans in terms of vegetation structure, composition and distance to water sources.

The effects of habitat manipulations on the abundance of herbivores could be weighed in relation to the objectives of the manager. This evaluation was done separately for each herbivore species. Habitat requirements of herbivore species included vegetation structure, vegetation composition, and the abundance of preferred food items. Additional criteria included cover from predators, cover for shade and proximity of water sources. I inserted different criteria in the program to help assess the importance of an animal species to the user of the program. Information for each animal species included current numerical status, conservation esteem, historic importance, and trophy and meat values. In this manner the user could prioritize the values of different natural resources in the reserve on a comparative basis.

The feasibility of bush clearance requires a careful evaluation of the environmental conditions and should also coincide with the objectives of the manager. Variables considered in the program included the available facilities for clearance, the viability of recreational activities, the local topography, soils, vegetation, large herbivore species and the combined effects of climate and burning.

I also designed the program to allow a balanced evaluation of the viability of the re-introduction of locally extinct species such as roan antelope in view of a potential improvement of local habitats following bush clearance. Questions were phrased in a manner to weigh the current features of the area under consideration against the general habitat requirements of the different ungulate species. For example, roan antelope are commonly found within habitats featuring open woodlands with tall perennial grasses. Under particular conditions, the program recommended the use of fire, which could be applied for the control of bush encroachment and encourage the growth of particular climax grasses, although the results may only become apparent after decades.

Private game reserves like
Sabi-Sabi cater for the up-
market traveler and offer a
unique experience in the
bush during a short visit.

A rare wild dog sight in the Bushveld. The congregation of vehicles around attractive sights may spoil the pleasure of solitude in the bush, although the problem is a lot less common in private game reserves.

Too close for comfort. Large predators are habituated to the proximity of vehicles. Nonetheless, people moving out of the frame of a vehicle alarm the animals to the degree that they may attack.

Using the program, the manager could indicate his financial constraints and the mechanical means at his disposal. In cases where financial and mechanical resources were limited but management objectives favored the attainment of an open woodland, the program would recommend a compromise regarding a burning regime. Such a compromise could only be suggested if preliminary habitat assessment quite clearly determined that current degradation was light and density of grass cover could provide sufficient fuel load for fire. If available information supported the use of fire to combat bush encroachment, the program would probably recommend not to perform bush clearance by mechanical means. The next step is to set the timing of burning. Prevailing conditions like season, weather, previous rainfall, fire-break maintenance, available manpower and the extent of burning in neighboring areas are effectively evaluated before the program recommends burning the area under consideration.

I had an opportunity to test the reliability of the program by following the clearance of two areas. In both cases there were indications of habitat degradation. In the one area, bare patches of ground were apparent and gully erosion occurred in some of the drainage lines, while encroachment of bush was still fairly moderate. The second area, on the other hand, showed advanced signs of degradation. Grass cover was depleted and sheet and gully erosion were evident, although there was no bush encroachment. Old aerial photographs were used as a reference, which indicated that the first area was a grassland with patches of woodland. The second area showed some signs of erosion for the past 20 years.

The program produced the following recommendations. Gully erosion should be treated and bush clearance should be conducted in both areas. The reasoning for clearing the second area was because the brush packing, or cover, protected bare patches of ground. This would prevent further soil runoff and create a favorable microclimate for the regeneration of grasses by capturing moisture. In view of the facilities at the manager's disposal, the program recommended the use of chain saws followed by a spot application of arborcides on stumps to prevent coppicing.

Two years later, I evaluated the effectiveness of the treatments. A partial success was achieved in the first area. The signs of degradation disappeared after the drainage lines were sealed and erosion was halted. Furthermore, tourists could observe grazers like wilde-

A wild dog is treated by the veterinary service of the Kruger National Park after it was found entangled in a snare set by poachers. Without treatment the wild dog would certainly have died.

beest and zebra in the area more frequently. However, coppicing of stumps was quite apparent and the area had to be re-treated during the following years, thus reducing considerably the economic viability of the initial treatment. The second area was more successful. Good rainfall and existing brush packing on bare soil patches were sufficient to recover grass growth. Game became quite frequent in the area and the tourist operation benefited from being able to use a

previously under-utilized portion of land. Furthermore, coppicing was halted, although it appeared that the arborcides in use were effective only against acacia species. The experience showed quite clearly that an appropriate technology for bush clearance should always take into consideration the features of particular areas (such as the composition of the plant species) coupled with local requirements in order to achieve an economic treatment.

A leopard is treated after being mauled by lions. There is a fine line between being humane towards animals and letting nature take its own course. Rightly or wrongly, large predators often receive more attention.

The Ultimate Wilderness –
Okavango Delta and Chobe National Park

The semi-arid savannas and the Okavango Delta of northern Botswana are among the few African wilderness regions that truly remain unspoiled. It is Africa and nature exposing its bare elements, wild and unforgiving. This makes mundane tasks, such as traversing a sand ridge or a muddy swamp, not to mention conducting scientific research, a mission. After the ecological enigmas of the Bushveld, I was eager to tackle a more fundamental issue, in this case the problem of the largest herd of elephants in Africa. The harshness of northern Botswana provided further challenge. Not only did I had to provide scientific evidence for the future survival or demise of elephants in the region, but I also had to cope with the hardships of daily life in the bush.

During the first days of my stay in northern Botswana, I traveled to the very northernmost area, shaped by the curving Chobe River with its deep, calm waters. The sight of animals was familiar and reassuring. Here, in between the bushes and

ANGOLA

ZAMBIA

• Livingstone

Zambezi River

NAMIBIA

KAUDOM GAME PARK

CHOBE NATIONAL PARK

ZIMBABWE

Okavango Delta

BOTSWANA

Mahalapye •

SOUTH AFRICA

Kalahari Desert

on the vast flood plains, impala browsed and buffalo made their way to the water's edge, trailing a column of dust that could be seen from far away. At night, the sharp and saw-like grunt of a leopard declaring its territory outside the tent could not stir me from sleep. I felt at home. By then, the experience I had gained helped me to overcome the daily difficulties without much hassle. I was able to pay much more attention to the wildlife and the subject of my research, the elephants. Elephants in northern Botswana wander over considerable distances to reach the Okavango Delta in their search for water and food. Although not many elephants stay permanently in this aquatic environment, the delta is a superb place to follow a diverse spectrum of animals, among which the fish eagle and wild dogs are perhaps the most prominent.

This was the ultimate combination. Not only are the animals effectively and enduringly protected, but also there was nobody else around. In a typical afternoon scene, after completing a data collection session earlier that day, I would be by myself, sitting on a log not far from a water source, watching monkeys playing, a mongoose foraging for food and the occasional elephant strolling by. I was completely immersed in the surroundings and the animals responded accordingly. That is, for most of the time I was ignored, unless one individual, be it an ant or an elephant, approached to investigate my presence. From time to time I acknowledged the dangers that lurked in the vicinity, such as a black mamba that slid past the base of a bush not far behind me. But fear did not dominate my thoughts. A tranquil fascination accompanied my thoughts and feelings throughout my time in the bush.

The Okavango Delta

A river delta that feeds a desert is something to consider. A delta that shatters the monotony and bleakness of an arid region with vivid contrast of colors and richness of wildlife, is something to behold. The Okavango River carries fresh, cool water from the highlands of Angola, providing 95 percent of all the surface water in Botswana and supporting a mosaic of wetlands, flood plains and reed beds that change with fluctuations in the water table. The Okavango Delta is a throwback to a huge lake basin that was at least twice the current size of the delta, and it is generally accepted that the basin is the southernmost tip of the Great Rift Valley. Movements in the earth's crust altered the elevation differences and, subsequently, the flow of water, so that now the fall in height of the Okavango Delta is a mere 62 meters across a distance of 250 kilometers from top to bottom. Several fault lines can be traced in the region that run on a general north-south direction, which means that even slight tectonic shifts can cause a dramatic change on the surface.

The volume of water in the Okavango Delta swells twice a year, although the duration, timing and amount of these rises differ annually. From November onwards, a rise in water level is expected and reaches a peak in late February. The greatest rise occurs at the top of the delta, an area also called the "Pan Handle" because of the shape of the delta as seen from satellite images. It may take six months before the peak reaches the bottom of the delta at Maun. The other rise is less predictable and is seldom noticed. It comes from water draining from the rains in northern Botswana and may cause flooding, particularly by the end of the rainy season in March.

The Okavango Delta drains to the Thamalakane and the Boteti rivers in southeast Botswana. After evaporation and percolation have taken their toll, these rivers receive a mere two percent of the volume of water that enters the delta. Even when it arrives from Angola, the water initially has a low sediment load, but the sluggish flow of water in the delta further purifies the water to become crystal clear. The water has a light amber coloration due to the suspension of fine organic matter and the presence of ferrous com-

Above:
Traditionally, mokoro were made out of sausage trees that have a strong timber which does not crack.

Pages 196–197:
Flock of white-faced ducks.

Previous pages:
Revenues from tourism gradually takes a larger share of the total income of local communities in the Delta.

ponents. It is a nutrient-poor environment and organisms scramble to utilize the small amounts of nitrogen compounds in order to survive.

The Okavango Delta is largely characterized by the dynamics of flooding and the formation of islands. Essentially, the delta can be divided into permanent and seasonal swamps. Permanent swamps have a dense growth of reeds and papyrus, and the water is covered with water lilies. The vegetation is evergreen and the environment provides a home for a rich variety of water birds, fish, crocodiles and hippos. However, it is the seasonal flooding that is probably the key to the diversity and richness of life in the delta. In a process that may take years to reach its climax, vegetation carried with the flow of water is trapped and gradually closes waterways. Reeds block further access of water and accumulate, thus creating a rich organic substrate. As the vegetation decomposes and piles up, plants that cannot subsist in an aquatic environment may establish themselves. Gradually, soil and sediments also accumulate and create a surface elevated above water level, thus forming an island. The island is then invaded by plants that are typically found on land and next to permanent river courses. The roots of the plants add further stability to the island and soil

may accumulate further. However, while additional material is constantly added to the periphery of the island, the surface level at the center of the island stays much the same, rather like a coral lagoon. While the edges of the island maintain the conditions for the development of plants due to the constant exchange of elements and ions between the free water and the trapped substance and soil, salt accumulates on the surface of the soil in the central part of the island. As the salt crusts on the surface, it changes the qualities of the substrate and renders further growth of plants almost impossible. Hence, viewing the islands from the air, it is possible to assess the current status and likely future development of each island.

The accumulation of vegetation results not only in the formation of islands, but also in altering the flow of water in the delta. Surprisingly, hippos play a principal role here. By creating well-trampled pathways in the swamps and on land, hippos facilitate the flow of water and increase the size of flooded areas. Up until 30 years ago, for example, the southern areas received a high proportion of the flow. Now it seems that the direction of flow has changed and is concentrated in the central parts of the delta. In addition, the dynamics of flood plains also change dramatically. Flood

Local villagers subsist on livestock and fishing in the rich waters of the Delta.

plains are the transitional stage between the dry land and swamp. Water floods the plains periodically and encourages the rapid growth of pastures and semi-aquatic plant communities that are favored by large herbivores such as red lechwe, reedbuck and water-buck. Buffaloes, zebra, wildebeest and impala, on the other hand, favor the new flushes of green on the edges of the flood plains. In turn, such a rich wildlife habitat also attracts a plethora of carnivores. With the change of flow, new flood plains are created and others dry out. The game, of course, moves with the flooding regime.

The Okavango Delta is within the jurisdiction of Ngamiland, an extensive region in northeastern Botswana. The word "Ngami" is a corruption of the Bayei word "Ncama," meaning "floating mat of reeds." Similarly, Maun, the largest town and the hub of tourist operations in the district stands for "the place of reeds." There is evidence of the migration of the Bayei and Hambukushu peoples some three centuries ago along the major drainage systems in the region. It seems that paintings on rocks north of the delta in Savuti, as well as in the Tsodilo hills in the southwest, were left by the Basubiya who followed the two tribes. The Bayei were the first of the Bantu-speaking people

Salt crystallizes on the shore of a small island in the Okavango Delta.

Opposite:
The delta that drains into the desert. Ninety percent of the water loss in the Okavango Delta is due to evaporation.

to migrate south of the Zambezi River. They subsisted mainly on fishing and hunting as the tsetse fly infected livestock with sleeping sickness. From the middle of the eighteenth century, the Bayei tribe utilized the waterways of the delta as highways on their migration routes. Among their means of transportation was the mokoro, the dugout canoe. The process of manufac-turing a mokoro used to be very time-consuming and required considerable skill – a single mokoro could take five months to build. The price was determined by the number of people the canoe could take before

Mokoro dugout canoes are the popular mode of travel in the Okavango Delta.

Traveling between islands in
the Okavango Delta can be
quite an experience for drivers
of 4x4 vehicles.

A pied kingfisher on a perch stalking fish in the water.

Stalks of water plants adorn an Okavango sunset.

sinking. Nowadays the mokoro is made from a fiberglass, although the original shape has not changed.

My first personal encounter with mokoro was not inspiring. I was with a group of graduates of zoology from Pretoria University on a trip to northern Botswana. We were a party of 20 people traveling in three vehicles, two of which were 4x4s. We assumed that we would be able to tow the minibus out of trouble whenever we came across deep, sandy patches along the road. By the time we arrived at the southern part of the delta, the two 4x4s had broken down. So we had to improvise and reverted to an aquatic trip on the mokoro. For several days we enjoyed the calm surroundings and the splendor of the diversity of birds in the delta. On the way back, however, the mokoro in which I was along with a classmate and a punter, and our bags, tipped over. I surfaced and saw my classmate and the punter swimming to the bank. The bags were already drifting downstream and our camp equipment with all our kitchen utensils sank to the bottom of the delta. I grabbed my camera bag and tried to hold it above water, although it was heavy and I struggled to get to the bank. The bank itself was muddy and slippery and I slid back into the water each time I attempted to get up onto it. Finally, I had to throw the camera bag onto the bank and with my hands free, I managed to climb up. Fortunately, the cameras survived and we rushed downstream and recovered the rest of the floating equipment. However, I was understandably reluctant to get back to the mokoro and walked the rest of the way to camp.

Today, most of northern Botswana is allocated for the protection of wildlife. While the northern part, Chobe, is proclaimed as a national park, the Okavan-go Delta has remained a tribal trust land where land is protected under the law and the local tribe takes an active role in the management of the land. As such, proceeds from hunting quotas and revenues from the lease of land to tour operators are shared between the government and the local authorities. It is a constructive approach to the conservation of natural heritage and resources, as locals have an incentive to keep the land free from harm for future generations.

However, progress takes its toll. With more efficient means to control the tsetse fly, it became finally possible to introduce cattle to the areas that border the delta. In an arid region, over-stocking had rather dire consequences on the natural vegetation and soils. As land became exhausted, it led to pressure to release additional land, which had initially been allocated to nature reserves. The long buffalo fence that separated cattle and wildlife accentuated the contrast between the overgrazed cattle land and the apparently lightly utilized wildlife areas. The buffalo fence was built in the early 1980s to keep buffalo and cattle apart, so that exported meat would meet the requirements and standards of the European Economic Community. The problem was that some ungulate species and buffalo in particular, are agents of the foot and mouth disease, although not bearing the symptoms themselves. Ironically, the fence did keep the delta from the invasion of livestock. However, it also epitomizes the conflict of interests and practices between the activities of man and the future integrity of natural systems only too clearly.

Dragonfly

Despite its name, dragonflies are not related to the common house fly and members of the fly family. Adults have slender bodies with large eyes that provide good vision. When capturing prey, or courting females, dragonflies demonstrate their flight skills in full to any observer who cares to sit and watch them by the edge of a pond or a small lagoon. They hunt by sight and seize their insect prey on the wing. The larvae are aquatic predators, feeding on small animals by shooting out the long, sharp appendages from the bottom part of the mouth. Their legs are relatively slender and form the shape of a basket when feeding, so that they can hold and feed from their prey during flight.

During mating, the male transfers semen from his genital pore to the accessory genitalia of the female by curving its abdomen until the two pores make contact. To do so, the male has to catch the female with his terminal appendages that resemble a pair of hooks. In many species, mating takes place while the couple fly around for a considerable time in a tandem position. Most females lay their eggs in the water, tapping the surface of the water with their abdomen to help release the eggs. The emerging larva transforms into a nymph. This transformation signals the beginning of a predatory life cycle. Prey is captured by the sudden, rapid release of the long clasps at the bottom of the nymph's mouth. The clasps are armed with teeth and spines that secure a grip on the prey. Larger nymphs prey on insects, tadpoles, worms and small fish. After several moults, the mature nymph climbs up stems of grasses or reeds where it sheds its last skin and becomes a soft and delicate dragonfly.

Crocodile

For all their fierce reputation, the few crocodiles that are spotted in African nature reserves do not live up to their myths and the legends. Hunted to the verge of extinction because of its reputation as a man-eater and for its hide, the sight of dozens of crocodiles basking in the sun on the sandy shore of a river is rare. Nonetheless, a mature crocodile is an impressive sight and certainly justifies the awe and indignation' that inspired ancient cultures. Albeit smaller, this reptile has not changed considerably over the course of evolution during the past 90 million years.

Crocodiles prey on fish, water birds and mammals. Stealthy in their approach, they are the masters

A little predator – a dragonfly hovers in search of prey.

Toads and frogs are commonly found in low places that are filled with moisture. The delicate skin of amphibians is prone to dehydration, thus forcing most of the species to seek the recluse of moist and shaded areas.

of ambush among the reptiles. The position of the nostrils and the eyes at the top of the skull allow the crocodile to remain completely submerged in water and yet scan for prey. When the crocodile dives, special valves seal the nostrils, ears and mouth while the eyes are protected with a third iris layer. Its lungs are perfectly adapted to remaining under water for long periods, and it propels itself forward with undulating movements of the body and the long tail as the legs are folded backwards.

Although most of the crocodile's diet comprises fish, some specialize in hunting mammals. At dawn, when ungulates congregate to drink, crocodiles ambush their prey from hiding places among water plants. They approach their intended prey carefully, but as soon as they get close enough, the crocodile virtually catapults from its submerged position using the powerful thrust of its tail. It grasps its victim and retreats to the water, where it secures its grip on the prey and drowns it.

In a shady corner, under the crowns of a tall riverine forest, along the Sabi River, there is a spot called Postman's Rest. It marks the location where the postman of Skukuza, the headquarters of the Kruger National Park, was wading through shallow water to a sandy beach to fish on his day off, and was taken by a large crocodile. Occasionally we went to swim in the Sabi River, not far from Postman's Rest. As security against crocodiles and hippos, we looked for rapids where their approach would be disclosed. My worry at

the time was more about the thriving bilharzia in the water than crocodiles. Later, when I stayed in the Okavango Delta, crocodiles and hippos were also a potential danger to swimmers who could not resist the inviting water. My favorite washing place in the delta was at a small, cozy lagoon where a tourist was killed by a large crocodile a few years before. The drag marks of human legs on the bottom of the lagoon were the only clue of the fate of the tourist, as the crocodile disappeared without a trace. Knowing that crocodiles are creatures of habit and will return, I took great care to verify that no crocodile was lurking in the water when I entered, although I never stayed in the water long enough for a hidden crocodile to approach.

Crocodiles are territorial, particularly during the breeding season. Males perform ritualized displays before engaging in fights with invaders to their territories. The nature of the response of a territorial male to an invader depends on the rank of the individual. A mature male without a territory will provoke a strong reaction from the territory holder by comparison to a young male that just wanders through the territory. If the invader does not retreat, a fight may ensue in which the males attempt to clasp the head of the opponent with their jaws.

A territorial male remains active throughout the breeding season, while other crocodiles congregate on sandy beaches and avoid any excessive expenditure of energy. Any receptive female is welcomed into the territory, and territory holding is highly regarded by

Crocodiles are common in the Okavango Delta. However, their shy nature keeps them hidden from sight.

females as male crocodiles without territories will not manage to copulate sucessfully with females.

The location of the nest is critical for the successful hatching of the young crocodiles, and will be chosen carefully by a female. It is usually an elevated, shaded sandy patch with a slight incline. The height above the water level is also critical as flooding drowns the eggs. The female digs the nest not far away from the water-front to facilitate access to water for the young hatch-lings. About 40 eggs are laid in one batch. The shell is strong, but softens toward the end of gestation. After the eggs have been laid, the female seals the entrance to the nest, but remains on guard for the duration of the three-month incubation period. The role of the female seems to be merely protecting the eggs from predation as she does not tend the eggs. A consider-able number of predators are attracted to this easily obtainable and protein-rich food source, especially the Nile monitor. Once a nest is exposed, however, other egg-eaters will join the feast, including marabou stork, ibis, heron, small carnivores and raptors. Other croco-diles are also major egg-eaters and are deterred from the vicinity of the nest by the female.

The hatching rate of crocodile eggs is normally high if the temperature and moisture content in the nest are suitable. After hatching underground, the young crocodiles call for assistance. The female ex-poses the surface of the nest carefully, as the sound of the young hatchlings attract other crocodiles as well as predators. Although active, the hatchlings require the assistance of the female to reach the water, who will carry them in her mouth and on her back. The mother has to keep up her vigilance after the young find their way to the water as large fish, such as cat fish, and herons will readily attack slow-moving young. Once hatched, the young remain in the same location for several weeks, and it seems that this is the only recog-nition cue for the mother as she cannot distinguish between her young and other batches of hatchlings.

The mortality rates of young crocodiles is extreme-ly high during the first days after hatching. A week after hatching, the young crocodiles gradually acquire survival skills and become more agile and present gap-ing mouths to potential aggressors. During their first seven years, crocodiles grow between 10 to 20 centi-meters per year. Sexual maturity is attained at approxi-mately 19 years of age.

Cattle egret

Cattle egrets are members of the large egret family, and are the least water dependent by comparison to its other members. Cattle egrets are often seen in the

The Okavango Delta is a haven for waterfowl and other bird species that favor wet habitats, like these egrets.

vicinity of large herbivores, hunting flies that swarm on the backs of herbivores and on top of fresh dung piles, or walking on the ground to catch the grasshop-pers that the herbivores flush as they move.

During the breeding season, cattle egrets flock in their thousands to areas of lakes and swamps, such as the Okavango Delta, where they establish dense breeding colonies and nest on the bare branches of tall trees. Some of the colonies are resident while others migrate between Africa and Europe, but the current distribution range is expanding because of the adap-tive nature of the birds. Cattle egrets also forage at rubbish dumps and do not hesitate to take advantage of man-made structures for nesting.

Fish eagle

The distinct call of the fish eagle is one of the symbols of Africa's wilderness. This beautiful bird is found on major river courses, lakes and estuaries and even the sea, if it can find its food. It may sit for hours on the prominent branch of a dead tree over shallow water waiting for fish to rise. The fish eagle then swoops down to take the fish close to the water surface, grasping the fish with its strong, curved talons and barely getting themselves wet. However, the eagle may also go underwater for its prey. More commonly, and unlike the noble images of eagles swooping with their talons stretched, eagles will eat stranded and dead fish.

A great white egret.

The coppery-tailed coucal produces a deep cooing sound, a beautiful wake-up call.

The Okavango Delta is a refuge for the rare wattled crane. The male on the right is courting a female by presenting her with grass stalks.

Occasionally, fish eagles may even harass smaller birds that have caught fish in an attempt to rob them of their bounty. They are often successful.

There are two ways to distinguish the male from the female of the species. The first is to measure the range of the wingspan. The female's wingspan reaches up to 2.44 meters, while the male only has a wingspan of roughly 1.83 meters. Another way to determine the sex of an eagle is to closely examine the form of the beak – females have deeper beaks, that is, the distance from the top of the beak to the chin is greater than that of the males.

Eagles mate for life although they will repeat the courtship flight every year they breed. Since eagles can live up to 30 years of age, they do not have to breed every year if the weather is adverse, there are not

enough suitable nesting sites or food is scarce. If conditions are favorable, fish eagles build enormous nest which they enlarge with each successive brood. Once an average clutch of two eggs has been laid, the pair alternates sitting duties during the 33 to 36 days of incubation. The young will leave the nest 10 to 11 weeks after hatching.

Many tour operators in Africa have tamed the local territorial pairs. The common practice is to call the eagle, which is most likely perched on its favorite tree, then throw a piece of fish into the water, not so close that the eagle will become timid, but not so far that the tourists will not be able to see the show. The fish is tied to a small stick to keep it floating. By and large, it is a mutual reward for the eagle and tourists – the problem is that the action is swift and unexpected,

A fish eagle attacks a pelican that has settled in its territory.

Opposite:
With its crop full of fish, a fish eagle leaps into the air.

and to get a decent photograph of the eagle in action can take up many spools of film. From a conservation perspective, the occasional fish serving does little to disturb the natural habits of these eagles.

Wild dog

Wild dogs, once considered ferocious predators, are nowadays among the most popular attractions in the African bush. They spend their entire lives in packs that vary in size from a couple of individuals to over 50, including pups. Wild dogs cover extensive distances in their search for prey, which ranges from small hares and gazelle fawns to adult zebra. In southern Africa, the most common prey for wild dogs is impala. They will not eat carrion and rely entirely on prey, mostly acquired through hunting in packs.

Wild dogs have extremely acute senses of smell, sight and hearing, and observing them at close quarters from open safari vehicles, one cannot help but notice their strong body odor. Since wild dogs are not territorial, the urine marking which is quite typical to most other members of the dog family is practiced only by the dominant female around the den, although when a couple is forming, the male usually leaves urine marks in tandem with the female, as if to proclaim ownership.

A pack consists of a breeding pair and a number of non-breeding adults that assist in looking after the breeding female and her pups. The sex ratio in a pack is often biased in favor of males, as they will remain in that natal pack whereas females inevitably emigrate once they have reached a certain age. In fact, the evolutionary development of a breeding pair and the social altruism among canids reach its apex with wild dogs. The species has specialized in the efficient utilization of abundant food sources through pack hunting and creating extended periods of dependence through large litters originating from one breeding pair. The breeding pair is at the top of two separate hierarchies of males and females in the pack. Casual observers will not notice the pecking order among the pack members as aggression levels in the group are very low. Submission takes the place of aggressive behavior as wild dogs rely entirely on cooperation for their survival.

Food sharing and cooperative hunting are continuously reinforced through behavioral patterns derived from begging at an early age. Greetings and submissive behavior are very common among the dogs. The pups utilize such behavior to persuade adults to share the kills. However, this privileged status is lost upon maturation and absorption into the hierarchy of the

With tails raised with excitement, wild dogs devour an impala they have just killed.

pack. However, handicapped adults which are unable to keep up with the pack will utilize submissive behavior to receive food.

Wild dogs bear around ten pups per litter. With such a large litter food becomes a limiting factor. It is therefore obvious, why only the alpha female can reproduce and successfully rear her pups. When a subordinate female breeds, the insistence of the dominant female on controlling the access to the pups prevents other adults from feeding the pups, and sometimes the alpha females will kill such pups. Males, by contrast, have an easier life in the wild dog society. They remain in the natal pack and maintain a pack of related males and one breeding and unrelated female. The maintenance of such a group structure prevents inbreeding in wild dog society. The alpha female remains with the pack into which she originally transferred and has a tenure of up to about eight years. The tenure of males is similar and may last a lifetime.

Food sharing and the regurgitation of food to pups are among the most exciting and moving scenes of the wild dog family, and is a prime example of the altruistic nature of their society. When the pups are more than a month old, they start supplementing their diet with meat provided by returning pack members. The pups solicit food by approaching an individual, chirping and thrusting their snouts into the adults' mouths. Adults that remained behind during a hunt are not prejudiced and also get a share of the regurgitated food. The social system of packs with overwhelming numbers of males by comparison to females is also an adaptation to ensure the survival of pups. The capacity of females to breed and rear the pups is the limiting resource in the pack. By reversing the roles and leaving much of the attendance of pups to males, the number of pups that can be raised successfully increases.

The size of the pack is the key to its future survival. Packs containing less than five adults may suffer greater pup mortality than bigger packs. Large packs fission when a subordinate female leaves with two or more males. The fission usually takes place when the alpha female is in estrus. Alternatively, males leave their natal pack if there are three or more litter mates. The males travel extensive distances in search of a new pack to join. Females, by contrast, are often seen with neighboring packs after they have emigrated. Normally, females stay in their pack until an opportunity to transfer occurs. Wild dogs avoid forming a small pack

Like all predators, wild dogs focus on their prey during the chase, regardless of obstacles they have to cross.

The Okavango Delta provides a refuge to a large number of wild dog packs.

because of the risk of being raided by foreign males that may abduct a breeding female.

Although wild dogs are efficient hunters with a sophisticated social system, they are on the decline throughout their distribution range in Africa. They are considered pests because of livestock predation and subsequently suffer from human persecution in rural areas. In the early 1960s, wild dogs were persecuted in national parks in Africa due to prevailing hatred and a common belief that herbivores should be protected from such vermin. Moreover, the later confinement of wild dogs to small nature reserves precluded them from finding a sufficient food supply. These factors brought the species to the brink of extinction. Yet, wild dogs are on the decline even in nature reserves that provide protection and sufficient food sources. For example, wild dogs in the Serengeti, Tanzania, that were much studied and photographed

quarry in sight, although they may also utilize moonlit nights for hunting. The most active periods of the day for the wild dog are in the early morning and late afternoon. Their hunting efficiency is high, and a pack may catch prey in the morning and evening of the same day. They rely on their endurance and maintain a speed of about 50 kilometers per hour for several kilometers. Mostly, one dog is seen closer to the intended prey and the rest of the pack trails behind with the immature dogs a long distance back. In southern Africa, it is very difficult to keep up with wild dogs hunting while on safari as the terrain where their favorite prey, the impala, is found, comprises of dense scrub. They move quickly and may change course without warning, following their prey. It is easier to keep up with the pace of the pups, who will always know where the pack is, and if they fall too far behind, one of the adults will trot back and reorientate them. However, by the time the pups arrive at the scene of the kill little is left on the ground.

The moment a quarry, such as impala, is over taken, it is grabbed and thrown onto the ground. Sometimes, the victim remains standing while the dogs have already disemboweled part of the stomach. With relatively small jaws and weak jaw muscles, a dog may have difficulty in overcoming a large prey. Nonetheless, through group effort, the prey is over-powered within minutes. Large herbivores, such as wildebeest and zebra, are formidable quarries and wild dogs will attempt to locate young individuals or single out an unfit individual. In a similar way to the technique applied by hyenas, wild dogs will openly approach herds, flushing game to identify suitable prey.

Since wild dogs are relatively small, many preda-tors attempt to rob kills from them. Hyenas, for ex-ample, will readily take over kills from small packs or packs protecting immature dogs. In some areas, a single hyena may satellite wild dog packs for a consid-erable time. The hyenas take advantage of the hunting success of the dogs and wait for the right opportunity to intervene. The dogs normally tolerate the presence of hyenas up to a point. On the fringes of the Okavan-go Delta, I frequently saw hyenas trailing wild dogs and moving onto their kill only after the wild dogs had consumed a large portion of the carcass. It seems that a status quo is achieved where the dogs ignore the hyaenas as long as they can consume most of the meat and thereafter attend their pups. The incredible hunt-ing success of dogs and high frequency of the hunts also encourages vultures to follow packs. Wild dogs consume only the meat part of the kill, leaving the skin and bones to the scavenging vultures.

during the 1960s suffered a dramatic decline in num-bers from which they have not yet recovered. The cause of the decline has not been thoroughly verified, but it seems that a combination of factors, such as severe competition with hyaenas for food, successive starvation of pups, flooding of dens and high suscepti-bility to diseases played a detrimental role.

Wild dogs are primarily diurnal. Hunting by day-light makes is easier for them to select and keep a

Waterbuck

Among the antelope that dwell in tropical and subtropical climates, the waterbuck is unique for its long hair coat and for being the most water dependent of all antelopes. Its coat of hair protects it from exposure to low water temperatures, although the water requirements of the waterbuck are such that it cannot withstand moderate exposure to heat without drinking. Like the lechwe, it favors vegetation near permanent water sources and at the first hint of danger will make for the sanctuary of water. It is a fast swimmer and gravitates towards deeper water where it is safe from terrestrial predators.

The waterbuck prefers firm, dry ground where it forages for grass. Low-lying areas with dense vegetation cover are usually avoided and the waterbuck can be found in open grasslands within a few kilometers from water. It is primarily a grazer preferring short- to medium-height grasses. During the dry season, when green grass with high protein levels is scarce, waterbuck revert to other types of forage like water plants and browse of shrub and tree leaves.

The rather patchy distribution of habitats suitable for waterbuck dictates to a large extent the form of social organization. Females associate in herds that have overlapping home ranges, but the herds vary in size and have no leadership or a ranking order. Females remain largely indifferent to other females that emigrate to the group and do not engage newcomers with grooming or other forms of physical

Opposite:
A male waterbuck poses in late afternoon light.

A male lechwe resting.

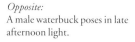

contact. Ultimately, the size of the herd is determined by the available resources. Waterbucks may reach high densities resulting in the deterioration of habitat, and emigration may take place voluntarily, if waterbuck exceed the carrying capacity of the habitat. Forceful evictions of individual waterbuck females are rare and are confined to weaned calves.

Male yearlings join bachelor herds where they stay until maturation. Unlike female herds, bachelor herds are closed to immigrants. However, no clear ranking is established within the herd. Bulls mature and establish territories by the age of six years old, quite a long time considering that males become sexually mature by the age of three. The territory is maintained year round and the tenure of territory holding is several years, depending on the location and attractiveness of the territory to female herds. The territorial bulls tolerate bachelor herds within their territories as long as the latter do not make attempts to mate with members of the female herds in the vicinity.

The occurrence of "satellite" males in the waterbuck social system is common. Satellite males are sexually mature bulls that do not establish territories and attach themselves to a proclaimed territory. They assist in defending the boundaries of the territory from invaders. However, such males will take some of the mating opportunities when the territorial male is absent or engaged. Satellite males enjoy the protection of a territory and also have improved chances of acquiring the territory when the incumbent dies or retires. Retired bulls do not return to bachelor groups but remain solitary.

Calf mortality is high in the first six months. Females prefer to conceal young calves, which follow their mother but often wander by themselves, making them easy prey for the spotted hyaena. Lions may prey upon adult waterbuck, concentrating on territorial males. Territorial bulls that are challenged by lions may confront the lions rather than flee.

Lechwe

The Okavango Delta is one of the strongholds of the lechwe in Africa. An aquatic antelope, it specializes in feeding on highly nutritious grasses that grow on inundated flats on the fringes of main waterways that are out of reach for most other antelopes. The lechwe can wade through water over extremely long distances and feed on vegetation while it is partially submerged in water. The movements of lechwe are very much determined by the tide and annual flooding regimes as they feed almost exclusively on grasses and sedges that grow in shallow water.

In the right habitat, lechwe can reach high concentrations. Resident populations like the one in Moremi Game Reserve on the edge of the Okavango Delta is divivded by territorial males into female and bachelor herds. Typically, females and their calves are nearer to the water than males which forage on the drier ground. The separation is partly an anti-predator strategy as females will seek the refuge of water to protect their young. Nonetheless, sexual segregation is maintained only during the breeding season where males compete for territories. Generally, the associations in female herds are loose and no leaders can be observed among the herds.

The movement of the lechwe is peculiar among antelopes. It runs with a bounding gallop with its chin outstretched so that the horns of the male lie parallel to the line of the back. Being a semi-aquatic creature, lechwe have adopted a fast method of getting through the shallow water. They make spectacular leaps, and upon the approach of a predator will jump in different directions. Lechwe typically retreat and flee into water if danger is imminent, as on land they would be out-run by hyena and wild dog. The range of predators for this medium- to large-sized antelope includes all the large carnivores, although calf mortality may also be a result of drowning.

The breeding behavior of lechwe males is unique in the sense that territories are established in the form of what are called "leks." These leks are small territories that the males maintain for a short duration because the flooding regime means that there are changes in the water level, and thus also changes in the distance to feeding sites. Because of the mobility of territory and crowding of lechwe, not only territorial males gain access to females but also males without a territory. Nonetheless, most females find males upon coming into estrus and mate with more than one male. The position of the arena of leks is on open ground near water that does not necessarily provide favorable pastures. As such, males tend to form conventional territories on waterfront areas if the distribution of favorable habitats is patchy. Subsequently, the expected levels of sexual activity and aggression between males are reduced to a large degree.

Opposite:
Red lechwe are found throughout the wet parts of the delta. A female demonstrates the jumping ability of the species in shallow water.

Wildebeest and red lechwe look intently towards a pride of lions (out of view).

Hippopotamus

Visitors to the African bush can usually expect to see only the ears, eyes and nostrils of a hippo, while the rest of its body is submerged in the dark water of a river. Hippos maintain an amphibian life style, spending most of the daytime submerged and emerging onto the land at night to feed. The shape of the hippo, bulky with short appendages and with its sensory and breathing organs at the top of the skull, are signs of adaptation to an aquatic environment. The water serves as a temperature control medium and carries the weight of the hippo. However, this adaptation is also the hippo's downfall. Since water serves as a body temperature regulator, convection from the surface of the skin to the surrounding water is high. As a result, the rate of loss of water under dry conditions is also high and leads to quick dehydration. Another characteristic of the skin is the absence of proper temperature-regulating sweat glands. Instead, there are glands below the skin that secrete a pink fluid that dries and forms a lacquer on the surface of the skin, vaguely similar to the processes that cause tanning in man. Hence, the function of the glands is to provide protection against the sun and against infections.

Powerful muscles which seal the nostrils and ears underwater mean that hippos are able to spend as long as ten minutes underwater without needing to surface for air. They can also walk easily on muddy surfaces, and despite their considerable bulk, one must never underestimate their speed and agility. They can outrun a man without much effort and are quick to respond to any sign of danger.

Previous pages:
Hippos in the shallow waters of an Okavango lagoon.

A threat display by a female hippopotamus settled in a canal, only a few meters away from a busy road.

Hippos feed almost exclusively on terrestrial vegetation and prefer species of short grass. Grazing is performed by a plucking movement of their broad lips. It is easy to recognize pastures that have been grazed by hippos by their well-mowed, golf course-like appearance. Food is digested in ruminant-like manner in a stomach divided into compartments, but the process seems rather inefficient. Nonetheless, for its size, the hippo consumes surprisingly small quantities of food, perhaps due to the fact that its inactivity minimizes energy expenditure.

In many wetland areas where hippos reach high densities, they serve an important ecological function, replenishing nutrient loss from land to water by removing grass and defecating in waterways. Through their massive biomass intake, hippos are able to alter habitats that they frequent, to the extent that overgrazing of pastures on the shores of lakes may cause excessive erosion and habitat destruction. Nonetheless, for most of the time, hippos enhance the diversity of the ecosystem. In the Okavango Delta, for example, hippos open up waterways that become clogged with vegetation and thus allow the rejuvenation of life forms living close to water.

The resonant honking call made by submerged hippos, which is used to express courtship and territoriality, is one of the most impressive calls made by African wildlife. Given their aquatic environment, hippos are restricted in their ability to communicate by means of sight and smell. Territorial bulls have ritualized encounters, and in addition, they deposit conspicuous dung middens that are found along hippo paths. Paths start at the water edge and lead out of and into the territories. Middens are most frequent near the shore, and are renewed nightly by bulls on their way to pasture. Before marking, a bull smells the existing deposit, then backs up and urinates and defecates, enhancing his excrement by tail paddling. It seems that dung showering is a form of dominance assertion, in addition to territory advertising. Even females and subordinate males tail paddle after turning away from an approaching dominant male. They may use this behavior pattern to avert aggression. Dominant males are highly aggressive and will not hesitate to attack juveniles and calves, often trying to kill them. Mothers normally keep the calves in nurseries and are savagely protective of their young.

Baby hippos are prone to predation by lions and crocodiles if not protected by their mother. A hippo's jaw is powerful enough to bite a fully grown crocodile in half. I witnessed the power of the hippo when I worked in a zoo. On one sunny winter's day, I was

feeding the animals on the shore of a large pond that was the sanctuary of several hippos. I was driving a tractor and a trailer, dropping alfalfa at designated points. I must have driven too close to the water's edge as suddenly a huge male came storming out of the water. It grabbed the front part of the tractor and was about to pull the radiator free. I drove the tractor forward, forcing the hippo to leave the radiator, and with a low grunt, he dashed back to the safety of the water. The tractor was safe, but I was shaken.

Perhaps surprisingly, the majority of human casualties caused by wildlife in Africa is the result of a hippo attack. Although a seemingly lazy animal, this impression is deceiving as the hippo is quick to respond aggressively to the approach of small boats and people who walk close to the water's edge. In particular, walking after dark close to waterways is extremely dangerous because of the likelihood of encountering hippos that have come out of the water for their nightly foraging.

A hippo makes a charge in response to an invasion of its territory by people.

The Okavango Delta is a haven for buffalo herds.

Right:
Cattle egrets forage for insects on the back of a buffalo.

A hippo herd is resting in the water while an African jakana forages for food between the slumped bodies.

Left:
A hippo emerges from the water in response to the approach of people.

Chobe National Park

Northern Botswana is flat, arid country situated north of the Kalahari Desert. Only four rivers are perennial, the Chobe, the Linyanti, the Kwando and the Okavango. Apart from the Okavango Delta, the inland area of northern Botswana relies on rainfall for its water, which even in good years is relatively low, while evaporation rates are high. The tributaries of the Chobe River that mark the northern boundary of Botswana are the Kwando and the Linyanti rivers, which flow along ancient fault lines. Where the Kwando bends almost at a right angle, it forms the Linyanti Swamp that gives rise to the Linyanti River. This is also the place where the Savuti Channel begins to make its way eastwards. When it flows, the channel spills into the Savuti Marsh, some 100 kilometers east of the Linyanti Swamp. The Savuti Marsh lies at the northern end of a large basin known as the Mababe Depression, a flat area covered with sparse shrub and grassland and bounded by sand ridges that were the shores of an old lake. The depression is fed by the Savuti Marsh in years when the Savuti Channel is flowing, and evidence suggests that it was once a vast lake and an integral part of the Okavango Delta. Nowadays, however, the elevation of northern Botswana's landscape through tectonic movements coupled with the deposition of sediments has altered the course of rivers and the formation of lakes, preventing a connection between the two basins. To the north of the Mababe Depression are the Gubatsaa and Gchoha Hills, among the few prominent land features in northern Botswana.

An aerial view of the dry land that stretches between the Okavango Delta and the Chobe River in the north reveals a mosaic of bush and scrub interrupted by patches of woodlands and grasslands. The vast expanse of this flat country gives a feeling of isol-

Previous pages:
The moon rises on the Savuti Marsh.

Opposite:
South of the Chobe River, a vast expanse of dry land is covered with a mosaic of shrubs and woodlands.

Sunsets during the wet season can be pretty if the cloud cover is not high.

ation and much of the aura of old Africa. Dry water courses can be made out, while evergreen riverine forests mark the permanent water courses. Isolated tracks appear coming from nowhere and ending nowhere. The tracks are well hidden in the vegetation, almost completely overgrown by grass. These jeep tracks are graded straight, marking the boundaries of Chobe National Park and stretching to the horizon, enhancing the eternal feeling that the landscape inspires. From the air, it is difficult to believe that the park is teeming with animal life. At low altitude, some elephants appear, resting under the shade of tall trees. Unlike East African savannas, large herds of herbivores are seldom seen. Most herbivores, such as zebra and wildebeest, appear in small herds that assemble only for short periods during the migration. It is only when approaching permanent water sources such as the Chobe River that larger concentrations of animals such as elephants and buffaloes come to view, as they make their way onto the river's flood plains.

Visitors that arrive in Savuti can tell right away when they are approaching the camp area by the sight of rocky outcrops, which are part of the Kgwebe formation and have high concentrations of quartz

feldspar. The intrusive rock formation that protrudes above the deep, sandy soil is similar in composition to the ancient Kalahari bedrock. This rock contains high concentrations of quartz that give rise to a large-grain, acidic, infertile soil. These soils contribute to the largest body of sand in the world. The sand is porous, which means that water percolates rapidly and disappears from the surface shortly after rain. The rainfall gradient increases in a northeasterly direction. Hence, while Maun, the tourist hub of the Okavango Delta, receives some 450mm per year, Kasane, the northeastern tip of Botswana receives more than 600mm rainfall per year.

Savuti is situated in the heart of the Chobe National Park. The reserve was proclaimed in 1961 before the independence of Botswana and was awarded the status of a national park in 1968, the year of independence. It is an unfenced reserve that borders designated hunting areas. The hunting areas serve as buffer zones between the fully protected reserve and the surrounding settlement areas. The park can be divided into three areas according to the concentrations of tourist facilities, with Savuti in the center, Serondella in the north on the bank of the Chobe

The Savuti Channel carried water from the northern Linyanti River up until the early 1980s.

Rain is a welcome relief in this semi-arid region.

The damp soil during the wet season attracts thousands of butterflies.

Previous pages:
The Chobe River front is the last place in Africa where the sight of large buffalo and elephant herds can frequently be seen.

Opposite, top:
Some butterflies quench their thirst by sipping the moisture from the dung of spotted hyena. A fly rests on the wings of the butterfly.

Opposite, bottom:
Hippos may venture to remote areas inland to enjoy the waters of seasonal pans while they last.

River, and the Linyanti in the northwest. The head-quarters of Chobe National Park is situated in Kasane, at the top end of the park. Game scouts are stationed at the various tourist camps and also have a mobile presence in their anti-poaching patrols.

Driving in Chobe requires the use of a 4x4 vehicle. The deep sandy tracks are a challenge to the skills of drivers and the mechanical sturdiness of vehicles. There are very few roads and tracks in the reserve, which means that if a breakdown occurs, it is, in fact, most likely that someone will drive past and provide assistance. However, due to heavy utilization of the roads, the sand is very deep and driving here is difficult, and the drive from Maun or Kasane to Savuti can take half a day.

In the Bayei dialect, Savuti means "unclear," referring to the irregularity of the flow of water in the Savuti Channel. Even when the channel is flowing, the Savuti Marsh is largely a dry grassland that erupts in green lushness roughly a month after the beginning of the annual rains. Because of the periodic flooding of the marsh, trees have little chance of establishing among the grasses. It seems, though, that since there have been long periods when the water flow was

interrupted, the lack of regeneration of woody plants in the marsh is not only related to flooding. Soil properties, competition for moisture from grass species and low annual rainfall also act against the establishment of trees. Dead acacia trees are a prominent feature of the landscape in the northwestern part of the marsh and along the Savuti Channel. It seems that during the previous dry periods, such as the one before 1957 that lasted for 70 years, the acacia trees established and attained full growth. When the channel resumed its flow, the water table level rose and drowned the roots – the trees subsequently died. Since the frequency of fire is rather low in the marsh, the tree skeletons remain to add to the eerie atmosphere of the place.

Other than near the marsh, fire is a common occurrence in Chobe, especially in the northern part. During the late winter months, fire sweeps through the park leaving only small and isolated patches of unburnt savanna. Most fires are induced by locals to encourage the growth of new grass for their cattle. Others initiate fires in the hunting areas, hoping to attract game to the fresh pastures. Some fires are initiated in Namibia and make their way all the way south across the border and the waterways that mark it. In

both cases, fire leaps across wide roads and tracks that serve as firebreaks and ravage the park for months until they are self-consumed. Moribund grass and dry leaves provide fuel for the fire, and habitats with long grass and more dry leaf litter enhance the intensity of fire and are more subject to the adverse effects of fire. Thus, Rhodesian teak woodlands that are common on the northern part of Chobe are more susceptible to the effects of fire. The best defense against a runaway fire is through back burning and scorching an area that is sufficiently wide and far enough in advance of the direction of the fire. The problem with back burning though is that it can get out of control and a change in the wind direction can mean that fire fighters have to cope with another source of fire.

In periods when the Savuti Channel is flowing, it provides an uninterrupted water source over a hundred kilometers. When flowing, the channel creates a remarkable contrast between the body of water and the surrounding arid landscape. This has dramatic effects on the resident animal populations. Animals that are dependent on water, such as buffaloes, congregate in large herds, and aquatic animals, such as crocodiles and hippos, venture inland to stay until the water recedes. The reverse happens when the channel

dries. Animals that are most dependent on water are the first to disappear. Gradually, the concentrations of game dwindle. If drought accompanies the drying out of the channel, the decline in animal numbers is rather dramatic as massive numbers of animals die from thirst and hunger.

Rains bring annual relief to the otherwise dry and desolate Savuti area. Throughout the year, the ground, plants and animals all wait in anticipation for the rains to come. Within days of the onslaught of the first rains, the grasses pump nutrients back to the dry and dying leaves. Trees that have already started to sprout leaves before the slightest indication of rain, blossom with shining green foliage. Shrubs that looked like dead scraps of branches, leaf and obscure the otherwise open visibility on the ground. The animals, no longer confined to the dwindling sources of water, scatter. At the start of the rainy season, water birds begin to flock to the vicinity of the marsh and the seasonal pans that are filling up. Hundreds of butterflies congregate around small ponds and on the moist ground. Ducks, herons, spoonbills, egrets, rollers, kingfishers and bee eaters fill the quiet air with their calls. Fish eagles and pelicans may also appear, much to the amusement of bird lovers that frequent

Savuti. The last of the rains should have fallen by th end of March, although the celebration carries on fo another month until the grasses shed their florescence As the grasses start to yellow and the pans dry out, animals dissipate to the sanctuary of the bush in anticipation of the coming winter period.

The change in seasons is a cue for large herbivores to migrate through the expansive dry land of northern Botswana. Elephants, buffaloes, wildebeest and zebra take the leading roles. The movements of wildebeest and zebra in the region were studied by my colleague, Mark Vanderwalle. He radio-collared animals and followed them using a micro-light aircraft. The primary purpose of the research was to probe the ecological factors behind the migration of those herbivores. In addition, Mark was trying to validate whether human-imposed constraints, such as fencing and hunting, have caused the decline in wildebeest and zebra numbers over the past decades. As might have been expected, the availability of surface water and nutritious pastures are the principal factors behind the large-scale movements of animals. Fortunately, although hunting takes its toll and fencing is prevalent in northern Botswana, these factors do not seem to hinder the populations of wildebeest and zebra con-

Previous pages:
Although many herbivores can extract sufficient moisture from their forage, they will not hesitate to drink if surface water is close. The approach of a bull elephant, however, indicates that the feast is close to its end.

Buffaloes edge towards the Chobe River before sunset.

Mopane trees form pure woodland stands on poorly drained soils in many of the dry parts of northern Botswana.

siderably. But why had the numbers declined? To start with, early assessments of numbers dating back to the 1960s were not reliable. However, no-one disputes that the trend for buffalo, wildebeest and zebra is downward. Personally, it seems that a combination of factors affects the animal populations. Among those factors, one can include consecutive years of drought, the long and collateral effects of fence construction and encroaching settlements.

Wildebeest and zebra drop their calves in the Savuti Marsh on their migration south to the Mababe Depression and into the fringes of the Kalahari Desert. The abundance of water and green pastures in the rainy season is a good time to drop the young, as the calves thrive on the rich milk that the mothers provide. During the months of December and January, the Savuti Marsh is teeming with herds of zebra and wildebeest and the air is full of the calls of zebra stallions herding their harems. This is also a prime time for lions and spotted hyenas. Hyenas scramble to capture foals and calves with their distended bellies nearly touching the ground. Lions prowl at night in their search for a fresh meal, and sprawl contented on the ground by the break of the following day.

The elephants in Savuti also have their annual cycle. Elephant bulls are permanent residents in the Savuti area, as the abundance of different habitat types that provide a variety of food sources, and the artificial waterhole sites that supplement the dwindling supply of water from natural pans, make Savuti a true haven. The movements of elephants in northern Botswana had been recorded by another of my camp mates, Dr George Calef. George and his wife, Brody, spent some seven years in Botswana while George was researching under the auspices of the Department of Wildlife and National Parks. He found through attaching radio collars that individual elephants had their summer and winter home ranges. Furthermore, elephants tend to come back to the same home range each year, some 200 kilometers apart. The movement of elephants in the region commenced from the perennial water sources in the north, such as the Chobe and the Linyanti, to the pans with mopane woodlands in the south and as far as the edge of the Kalahari, at Nxai Pan National Park. Surprisingly, in the dry and hot climate of the region, rain water may be held in pans for relatively long periods, well into the winter season under average rainfall conditions. Yet, after August,

During more than a decade that this pride was followed in the Savuti area, none of the lion cubs born survived to adulthood.

few, if any, pans remain to fulfil the requirements of elephants. Thus, in a normal year, elephants are obliged to leave the sanctuary of the mopane woodlands in the south and start their journey to the north by the end of July.

Mopane

Mopane woodlands dominate much of the savanna areas in northern Botswana as they thrive on poorly drained soils where many other tree species, such as acacia, succumb. Mopane grows in the form of trees and shrubs. It seems that the water-retention capacity of the soil determines the height of trees. In soils with high clay contents, trees may develop whereas the appearance of shrubs is indicative of a porous soil substrate. The root system of the mopane is shallow and adapted to the fast collection of water from recent rains that accumulate in a water-retaining clay horizon close to the surface. The numerous pans that form in the clay soils of mopane woodlands attract large numbers of animals, herbivores in particular, during the wet season. In addition, herbivores favor the grass species that grow in mopane woodlands. The young leaves of the mopane are also a nutritious supplement to the diet of herbivores. During the wet season, herbivores such as wildebeest and zebra concentrate in the mopane woodlands in the south of the northern Botswana region, including the Mababe Depression

and down to the edge of the Kalahari Desert on the vast expanse of the Makgadikgadi pans. As the water dries up in April, animals migrate back north to the permanent water courses in the north and the adjoining flood plains with tall grass growth.

The pattern of movement of elephants is similar to those of wildebeest and zebra. However, since mopane leaves are a principal food item in the diet of elephants, they are more closely associated with mopane woodlands than grazing herbivores. Elephants utilize mopane particularly during the dry season when other tree species become unpalatable as a result of nutrient absorption from leaves, deciduous properties, or the accumulation of high concentrations of tannins in the leaves. Tannins inhibit digestion in herbivores and are mostly present in leaves of trees and shrubs, as opposed to grasses. Tannins and other related compounds of aromatic oils produce pungent smells and defend plants against insects. While tannins are present in mopane leaves, it seems that the concentrations are not high enough to offset the nutritional value of the leaves. Elephants feed on the leaves, stems and bark of mopane. Thus, superficially, the level of destruction of an elephant herd visiting a patch of mopane woodland leaves room for doubt about whether the plants will recover. Nonetheless, mopane trees are resilient and have a remarkable capacity to recover from damage by both elephants and fire. New

A fungus grows on the dung of elephants which is partially submerged in the water of a pan.

shoots appear on top of fallen branches, some of which may in due course grow to the size of trees. Furthermore, the establishment of seedlings is less dependent on particular rainfall regimes and may take place in years of average rainfall. All in all, the effect of elephants on mopane are largely confined to the modification of vegetation structure, namely the conversion of tall woodlands to shrubs, under extremely high elephant concentrations.

The butterfly-shaped leaves of the mopane are both pretty and practical. When the leaves fold together and hang vertically, water loss is limited through minimizing the exposure of the leaf surface to the sun. Hence, mopane trees are not a good spot for shade in the middle of the day. Mopane seeds have a sticky balsam that adhere to the hooves of large herbivores that in turn transfer them elsewhere. The wood of the mopane is heavy and provides excellent charcoal for the camp fire. Moreover, the wood is a popular building material among locals who favor the straight trunks and appreciate its termite-resistant qualities. The tree also tends to form holes that provide an ideal habitat for tree squirrels, hornbills and woodpeckers.

Although serene and quiet on cool winter days, mopane woodlands may not be the ideal place to relax. An insect that associates with mopane trees, called the mopane bee, is a source of constant annoyance. These minute black bees are stingless, but their defense strategy is to buzz around the face. They are particularly attracted to the moisture around the eyes and the nose and are very persistent and irritating. Their nests are located in a hollow tree trunk with a concealed entrance formed by a tiny wax tube that protrudes from the tree trunk. During the course of fieldwork in mopane woodlands, I found that the best way to cope with the mopane bees was simply to ignore them. Alternatively, I used to take off my shirt and provide the bees with a much larger source of moisture. However, some of my dedicated assistants were not in a position to follow, with the result that I had to complete the work by myself.

Baobab

This magnificent tree adds much to the diversity of the African landscape. The origin of this name is the Egyptian name "Bu hobab," given to it by merchants

Mopane, a favorite food of elephants, is characterized by its butterfly-shaped leaves.

Baine's Baobabs at sunrise.

who traded in African products in Cairo during the seventeenth century. An apt description of the baobab was given by Dr David Livingstone, who referred to it as a giant upturned carrot. This term gave rise to its colloquial name of the upside down tree.

Many large baobabs are hundreds of years old. There appears to be a difference of opinion with respect to establishing the age and the potential lifespan of the species. Carbon-dated records indicate that baobabs with a five-meter diameter are around 600 years old. However, variable climatic conditions in different regions where baobabs occur account for considerable variations in the estimation of age according to the diameter of trees. For example, in times of drought, the girth of the trunk may actually contract. In addition, growth rates may differ and it appears that baobabs grow rapidly during the first 270 years of development, reaching a girth of approximately two meters.

The wood of the baobab is soft and spongy, and the moisture content of green wood may be up to 75 percent. Because of this rather high moisture content,

baobabs are susceptible to damage caused by elephants. During times of drought, elephants seek out the moisture in the bark by boring inside the wood. Since the baobabs are slow-growing trees, elephants can destroy a mature tree several centuries old in one season. Due to the sparseness of baobabs throughout most of their distribution range, there is a potential ecological imbalance that threatens the future of the trees. However, although elephants have the capacity to inflict heavy damage and alter the survival rates of baobabs, it seems that their impact is not severe because their diet requirements are far more diverse than that which baobabs can offer.

The baobab attracts a wide variety of animals, some of which stay permanently in the vicinity of the tree. Bees establish their hives in the crevices of the trunk, and pollination is influenced by a species of fruit bat that has a distribution range which coincides with the distribution of baobab trees. Baobab flowers bloom for 24 hours only and produce a stinking odor which attracts large number of insects that also play a role in the pollination process. Many trees become

hollow as a result of inner sap dying and the healing of the bark that curves around the empty insides. Hollow crevices in baobabs also serve as a water reservoir and attract small mammals and even tree-climbing carnivores such as genets and leopards. Many bird species nest in the trunk recesses.

Baobabs are also highly valued among locals throughout Africa, to the extent that people may trade with baobabs as assets. Bushmen utilized baobab bark for medicinal purposes and as a source of moisture, using fluid extracted from the trunk to dilute milk. Because of the soft wood, baobabs are an easy tree in which to pin pegs made from hard wood in the bark and climb up to bee hives for honey. The pulp and seeds are sources of nutritional food, while the leaves, when fresh, can be eaten as spinach. The shoots of germinating seeds are used as asparagus, bulbs and ends of roots can be used to make porridge, and the ash from burnt wood can even serve as a substitute for salt.

The Savuti Camp

Living in the bush is certainly a unique experience. It is a place of extremes and little compromise. The romantic aspect of living in the African bush is frequently interrupted by the burden of daily chores. General comforts of urban life, such as water from a tap, electricity, heating, cooling and even privacy, are precious commodities. Insects buzz and hover all over the place, particularly in summer. Nonetheless, the quality of life is enhanced by the daily contact with the indigenous creatures of the bush. Thus, to be able to enjoy life in the bush, one has to accept the austerity and thrive on the pungency and thrill of the experience of living outdoors.

A daily routine would start at dawn, the time of change of shifts when the air is cool and crisp and the nocturnal creatures are retreating to their hiding places. For those who cannot wake up, the francolins with their loud calls hint that it is about time to get up. Although up and about, I rarely did research work in the early hours of the morning. It is a precious time to watch animals and capture photographic opportunities as the light dapples on their skins and on the ground and trees. By the late hours of the morning, the magic is gone. The harsh light and the intense heat then creep in. This is the best time to get started with the daily activities that involve fieldwork or maintenance work in the camp. There is always something to fix and patch up from the activities of the night before. The maintenance of the vehicle is essential as it simply constitutes a matter of life and death.

Fighting against the elements is a full-time job. Dust gets into the tent and settles on beds, food and sensitive equipment. The rain penetrates the covers

Elephants were frequent visitors to the camp in Savuti.

Some of the camp residents were relatively harmless, like these yellow-billed hornbills that peck at their reflecting image on the windshield of the vehicle.

vehicle. The rain stopped and I vaguely heard some voices coming through the foliage. I could not open the door. I slowly crawled out of the open window and through the foliage to emerge among some Africans who had formed a circle around the scene. They thought that I was dead. It was only two days after the event that we finally managed to recover the Landrover from under the fallen trees.

There were few occasions, however, when I stayed in camp in the afternoons, when activities of the animals resumed. Elephants were congregating at the waterhole and lions were getting ready for the night hunt. After returning from a game drive, the evening meal was prepared over the campfire. There was not always something interesting in every game drive. After all, the bush is a quiet and calm place where the peaks of the struggle for survival are sudden and subside rapidly, sometimes without leaving a trace.

Sitting in company around the campfire after a good meal and listening to the sounds of the bush is a wonderful experience. Conversation is repeatedly interrupted with the roars of lions and the whooping calls of hyenas. The shadow of a prowling hyena disappears behind the bush and the monotonous call of a scops owl can be heard. Later at night, activity subsides. The bush and the camp fall silent. A rustle in the grass reveals the approach of a leopard. All the animals, except for the crickets, fall silent. The lions found their prey. The elephants had their drink.

The serenity and calmness of the bush are in many respects deceptive. True, nothing much is going on, particularly in the middle of the day. Nonetheless, dangers are lurking as animals do not distinguish between the camp grounds and the surrounding bush. Tragic encounters with animals in the camp are always accidental. However, it is complacency, inspired by the close proximity of comfortable commodities, which is the worst of all enemies in the camp site. Snakes escape detection by the ever-vigilant tree squirrels, francolins and hornbills, and settle in the cool corners and hidden places in the tent. They find their way to the shower in search of toads and the kitchen is also visited by snakes because of the presence of rodents. Field mice manage to pierce the packages of food and even make nests in metal trunks and cupboards. At night, lions walk past on their way to the waterhole. Lions were never a problem, although in some camps fatalities have occurred as a result of people wandering at dusk and at night without making themselves obvious. Lions are also dangerous to tent residents who leave the flaps of the tent open at night. Curiosity drives the lions inside and the cover

and fly sheets that protect the tent. Fortunately, as the rains come in summer, the sun soon appears behind the clouds and dries the tents. However, the roads remain muddy to the extent that we often got stranded for several days after a heavy storm. I tried to avoid staying in the bush at the times of rainy season both because of the muddy roads and the occurrence of malaria. One rainy day, I was sitting in the warm cabin of my Landrover, typing data into the computer. The rain was falling hard on the roof and the wind was blowing. Suddenly, without warning, I was engulfed by green foliage as a tree fell on top of the

of night makes them bolder. When the residents wake up, the lions instantly feel cornered and respond aggressively.

Elephants may also become a pest to the residents of the camp. Seeing an elephant browsing casually in the camp makes one feel part of the bush scene and not an intruder. Elephant bulls in Savuti had a long and enduring association with camps and their residents. Ever since the Savuti Channel dried in the early 1980s, they became reliant on the artificial waterhole. However, having been conditioned to the daily supply of fresh water, the resident elephant bulls were reluctant to leave. Knowing that the source of water rests with people, the elephants diverted their attention to the various camp sites in Savuti. I was not too worried, because their attempts to find and uproot the water pipes were hesitant and I was able to chase them away without much difficulty.

One night, however, I realized that there was one bull that was persistent in his attempts to tear and break the pipes. Late at night, I woke up to a loud bang. The elephant had broken the shower facilities of my neighbor. I rushed out of the tent and run into trouble. Unlike the docile habits of most elephant bulls in the area, I was promptly attacked and had to jump away fast. He came for the second attack and I took a handful of sand and threw it at his eyes. It worked and the bull stopped promptly. Moving sideways to reach a shrub, the elephant accidentally hit the tall radio antenna mast of the camp. The antenna came down crashing on the elephant's back. He became even more furious and stumbled on the poles and rocks that secured the antenna. Steel cables whistled through the air and I had to duck to avoid them. The elephant vented his anger on the remnants of the antenna and a shrub and then pushed off. The next morning, he was back and the ordeal was becoming a nightmare. I caught him when he was probing the structure of the shower, looking for moisture. I grabbed a large metal washing bowl and, despite the fact that it was a ridiculous attempt, threw it at his head. The bowl settled squarely on his forehead and stayed there for a second. Finally, the elephant grabbed the bowl with its trunk and threw it to the ground. He then trampled and twisted the bowl and turned it to a flat tin sheet to demonstrate its strength. His demand and need of water, however, did not cease.

Over the coming days and nights, the elephant came back repeatedly. Other elephants had given up and wandered off to places with water. The bull and myself developed a routine. He would hover around the premises of the camp waiting for the opportunity to approach the shower. Like a ritualized Spanish bull fight, I would confront the elephant at some stage and he would attack in response. Avoiding the elephant was not too difficult. I would wait until the very last moment and dart sideways while he carried on straight. He was waiting for me to stumble and fall, so that he could turn and finish the job. Fortunately, Mark and Sandra, my camp neighbors, came back to the camp from leave. They were not impressed by the presentation of bull fighting and Sandra indicated that eventually I would trip. She was right. The following night, I did not go out of the tent when the bull went

It is always a good idea to watch where you step. A puff adder snake hides beneath the entrance flap to the tent.

The front part of my vehicle protrudes under the foliage of fallen trees.

Below:
Banded mongoose take an interest in the stew pot.

to the shower. A loud bang from the direction of the toilet early the next morning indicated a change in the balance of power. The bull had broken the drain cover of the toilet. We decided there and then that the elephant could have the toilet while we retained the shower. Two weeks after the break, the waterhole was reopened. The elephant stopped visiting the toilet and we started with the repair work. For a few weeks thereafter, I saw the elephant coming to the waterhole. I never observed his fellow elephants greeting him upon his arrivals to the waterhole. Indeed, the other bulls seemed to stay away from him.

Chameleon

In the eyes of many Africans, the chameleon is a bad omen. With eyes that move independently and its changing body coloration, it is easy to understand how the myths arose. At the same time, the legends left the chameleon free to concentrate on hunting its favorite prey, insects, without interference. Indeed, for

slow-moving creature such a task is quite challenging. The independent movement of the eyes enables the chameleon to assess the distance to its prey, and at the same time watch for enemies. When it gets close enough to the prey, its long, sticky tongue strikes out at lightning speed. Meanwhile, the capacity it has to change its body color and blend with the surrounding foliage is an effective anti-predator mechanism, coupled with slow and calculated movements.

Chameleons inhabit different habitat types ranging from forests to arid areas with scant vegetation cover. In savanna areas, chameleons are hidden in the thickness of scrub and bush where they are active during the day. Like many other reptiles, the level of activity depends on the ambient temperature. As long as the temperature is low, the metabolic rate remains low. Nonetheless, through minimal loss of water, the chameleon can subsist in hot climates. The rate of color change on the skin depends on the current metabolic rate as well as the background color and the mood of the chameleon. While hunting, the chameleon moves slowly while swaying its body to the movements of the branch it is standing on. Its front leg has three digits on the inside and two on the outside. The arrangement on the hind legs is opposite. The tail is strong and functions like a fifth leg, holding the weight of the body. Most chameleon species lay eggs in a hole that the females dig in the ground or a hollow chamber in a tree. It seems that the female lays eggs only once in her lifetime.

Puff adder

Widespread in southern Africa, the puff adder accounts for the majority of the venomous snake bites in the region. It is a sluggish snake that relies on its cryptic colouring to escape detection. For this reason it is a very dangerous snake as victims are often bitten before they are aware of the snake's presence.

The puff adder belongs to the family of vipers which is the most developed in the order of snakes. It is a nocturnal snake, preying on small mammals, birds, amphibians and reptiles. During warm weather,

Simplicity dominates life at camps, with the evening campfire having a prominent role.

puff adders feed as much as they can to build up fat reserves for the dry, cold winter. When disturbed, it inflates itself and lets the air out in a loud hissing noise or puffs. Its sluggishness is deceptive as when striking, it moves very fast, forward or sideways, recoiling immediately and resuming a defensive position. While striking, the mouth is wide open, exposing the curved fangs in the front of the upper jaw. The fangs are erected as the mouth is opened due to a tendon attached to the base of each fang. Unlike other snakes with back fangs, the puff adder retreats after striking and does not keep hold of its prey. Their venom is not as deadly as that of the mamba and cobra and is mainly hemo-toxic. It induces internal bleeding from the mucous surfaces and extensive hemorrhage through the breakdown of red blood cells and the diffusion of blood into tissues that result in severe swelling.

I was fascinated by these snakes and their perfect camouflage during the early days of my stay in the bush. Needless to say, I was tempted to handle these seemingly sluggish creatures for the sake of taking better photographs. At one time I was holding a puff adder and carrying it to a suitable location with lots of dry leaves that blended better with its color. While holding the snake, I examined the snake's head. To my utter amazement, one of the fangs was already touching my finger. I had not been aware that the fangs can be rotated from their resting position even with the mouth closed. Opening my fingers, I inadvertently let the snake drop to the ground. The snake remained unhurt and retreated in haste into the bush. Since then, I have not handled any snakes. If a puff adder was discovered at camp, we would carefully guide the snake into a box and take it for a long drive.

Opposite:
Large African pythons are rare as they are caught by locals who sell the skin and internal organs to make traditional medicine.

When disturbed, the color of the chameleon changes to bright orange.

A yellow-billed hornbill is enjoying a feast as butterflies congregate.

Guinea fowl

The guinea fowl is a favorite game bird for Africans, although, as one African commented to me, the meat of the guinea fowl is tough because they walk too much! Visitors to game reserves and rural areas may see dozens of guinea fowl crossing the road on their foraging excursions. Guinea fowl walk several kilometers during the course of a day, feeding primarily on seeds, small seedlings and invertebrates. During the early morning, hundreds of guinea fowl can be seen drinking from a waterhole, while at dusk they flock to roosting sites on the branches of large trees.

The guinea fowl is a relative of the chicken and pheasants. Their body structure, however, is more robust with a short tail and naked head and neck. They are weak flyers, and if chased or harassed, they prefer to run away and will take flight only if they really have to. The female lays between 6 and 15 eggs in a small depression on the ground. Some Africans raise guinea fowl, but the egg output is low and they do so mainly for the meat. In addition, guinea fowl may serve as quite an effective early warning system on farms of rural areas, although they are noisy creatures to have at close quarters.

Yellow-billed hornbill

A common resident of camp sites in southern African savannas, the yellow-billed hornbill is a clumsy flyer that alternates wing flapping and gliding while flying. It feeds mainly on insects such as grasshoppers, caterpillars, termites, wasps, beetles, as well as small birds, chameleons, fruit and seeds. They become tame quite easily and will follow camp residents in the hope of sharing scraps of food. Hornbills sometimes show remarkably intelligent behaviour – in Savuti, for example, yellow-billed hornbills would admire their reflected image on the windscreens of vehicles for many hours. Many other bird species peck their own images, if they are presented with a mirror, assuming that they are encountering an intruder to their territory.

Cape turtle doves form large
flocks in the vicinity of waterholes during the dry season.

Right:
Guinea fowl arrive at waterholes during the early hours
of the day.

A male masked weaver builds its nest at the end of a low hanging branch, as far away as possible from the reach of snakes.

The lilac-breasted rollers nest in natural holes in trees.

Black-shouldered kite

The black-shouldered kite has a disrupted distribution range throughout Africa and Asia. It has a relatively small beak, wide at the base and compressed at the tip. Black-shouldered kites have short legs covered with feathers and bare toes. They are common residents of fairly open country with scattered clumps of trees and bush, nesting on low trees and sometimes using the nests of other birds of the same size.

Unlike eagles and vultures, this kite does not soar to any height. While hunting, it hugs the ground during the course of flight, maneuvering sharply and hovering. As it hovers and detects a potential prey, the kite will raise its wings for several seconds, lose altitude and then resume hovering at a lower height. Finally, with outstretched talons, it will drop on the unsuspecting prey below.

Giant eagle owl

The giant eagle owl is among the largest owls in southern Africa. It is a resident of woodland savannas with large trees. During the day, this owl will perch on large branches and appear at dusk on conspicuous posts, uttering characteristic calls. By comparison to other owl species, the giant eagle owl differs in the larger prey size that it is able to capture, taking hares, vervet monkeys, guinea fowl and other birds up to that size, but also smaller prey, such as fruit bats and insects. I suspect that most yearling hornbills in the camp at Savuti fell prey to the local giant eagle owl.

Martial eagle

The martial eagle is the largest eagle in the southern African savannas. Its beak is strong and curved, and is

Having caught a rodent, a black-shouldered kite tightens its grip around the prey before flying away.

A group of marabou storks roost while elephants forage in the distance.

Opposite:
A martial eagle relaxes after catching a guinea fowl.

Following pages:
The crop of the marabou stork may be utilized for cooling by driving air through the sac.

matched by its strong legs and well-developed talons. They choose prominent vantage points early in the morning, where they can observe the movements of potential prey. Upon the sight of a suitable prey, the eagle virtually throws itself on the prey with a fast flutter of wings. The speed of the swoop is incredible. It can be photographed only if the photographer is well prepared and spends a long time watching the eagle and waiting for an opportunity. As the morning progresses, the eagle may soar high in the air without moving its wings. If prey is spotted, the eagle folds its wings and dives almost vertically on its prey. A few meters before reaching the prey, the eagle spreads its wings to reduce speed while avoiding ground obstacles. It hits the prey with its legs, sinking its talons in for a tight grip.

About two thirds of its diet is made up of birds, guinea fowl being the favorite species. Francolins and korhaans are also commonly taken. Occasionally, martial eagles will hunt small mammals, such as rock hyrax, hares, dik-dik and steenbok. Equally, Impala and springbok fawns are not rejected if found. Given

the opportunity, martial eagles will also hunt small jackals, servals, mongooses, storks and snakes.

Marabou stork

These ugly-looking birds undeservedly gained a bad reputation from hanging around rubbish dumps and sharing the spoils of carcasses with vultures. Yet, marabou undeniably fulfill an important function in the savanna ecosystem through consuming carrion meat and facilitating nutrient cycling. Interestingly, vultures are respectful of the marabou because of its long and powerful bill. In flight Marabou storks look rather majestic, soaring in the sky with a wingspread of up to 2.60 meters. In a similar way to many vulture species in Africa, marabou storks also nest on tall trees. However, unlike them, the diet of the marabou is not restricted to carrion meat. They also stalk insects on the grass plains, and may also occasionally eat reptiles and amphibians. In Etosha National Park, for example, marabou storks were photographed as they were hunting mourning doves that dropped to the edge of the waterhole to drink.

Baboon

Baboons monopolize the niche of a true savanna primate in that they are capable not only of arboreal foraging, but also because they will not hesitate to venture out into open grassland far from the safety of shelter. It is a highly opportunistic primate which eats a diverse range of plant species and animals. Early in the rains, a troop of baboons may restrict itself to feeding on sprouting grass. Late in the dry season when food becomes scarce, they will dig out rhizomes and bulbs. Any insect dug out in the process also makes a good dietary supplement. In addition, baboons will readily eat lizards, frogs and ground-nesting birds. However, they are confined to areas that have surface water and safe sleeping sites such as tall trees and high cliffs. They do have a limited ability to extract moisture from their food, and supplementary water is required, particularly by young members of the troop.

Baboon troops occupy home ranges that overlap with other troops. Troops tend to avoid one another even though at times they are required to share limited resources like surface water and roosting places. Females constitute the stable core of the troop. They remain in the troop for their entire lives whereas males emigrate and may transfer repeatedly between troops. Nonetheless, a stable hierarchy characterizes the social organization centered around females and their offspring. Ranking is related to female lineage and by the age of three, the rank of a juvenile female is already determined for life.

Juvenile males remain in kinship groups and are subordinate to the females until maturity. In adolescence, males experience a rapid phase of growth. Having become larger and more powerful than females, males may dominate the elder females. Shortly thereafter, however, males will start to transfer between troops. Dominance and reproductive success are linked in males. Females are receptive to dominant males, and in particular to newcomers to the troop. Therefore, it is advantageous for a mature male to emi-

Opposite:
In northern Botswana, baboons often became pests at the camps, having learnt that food and water are easily obtained here.

Grooming is an important ritual in baboon society.

grate to a new troop. Nonetheless, pair bonding is also a prominent feature in the baboon society, and males have to cultivate relationships with particular females prior to mating. Males that manage to establish associations with particular females take care of the female's offspring through holding, carrying, grooming and food sharing. These "godfathers" go as far as becoming foster parents to juveniles whose mothers die.

The communication patterns of baboons are quite advanced and complex. It is easy, for example, for a human observer to identify with the behavior of individuals. Facial expressions are combined with body language and vocalization to provide subtle cues and a rich form of communication. For example, when a subordinate member of the troop passes close to a dominant member, a fear grimace may appear on its face. In addition, the baboon may flatten its ears and emit a yakking sound if they are afraid. Like other monkeys, tactile communication plays a major role in their lives. The complicated network of relationships, associations and ranking order can be deciphered by observing the individuals that groom and the way they do it. Grooming is the first activity conducted in the morning after sleep, with the direction of grooming from lower to higher rank, except for mothers and their infants. Males receive more grooming than they give and individuals may be tense or relaxed while grooming depending on the difference between rank.

Aggression in the baboon troop varies according to variables such as the presence of another troop, as well as the balance of the relationships between individuals in the troop. Troops with new male immigrants or newly matured males tend to be rather unstable and display more aggression. Most confrontations do not end in serious injuries, in spite of the large canines that males possess. Yet, males may bear scars on their heads from past fights. Teasing or bullying of small baboons by older individuals, or squabbles between females, frequently lead to chases and loud shrieks. Individuals that are caught are bitten or slapped. Nonetheless, the duration of such chases is short and resulting injuries are rare. Similarly, confrontations and aggression between troops vary according to the degree of competition for scarce resources and the degree of relatedness, in terms of the number of males that have transferred to the opposition troop. Males take the lead in such disputes, but there is rarely a physical contact. Frequently, the troop with the larger number of males wins such confrontations.

Female baboons give birth to helpless infants that require intensive care. An infant baboon gains locomotion skills by the end of its first month. Until then,

the infant clings tightly to the bosom of the female in a ventral position. From then on, the growing juvenile rides in the jockey position although some baboons never change from the ventral position. By their fourth month, baboons acquire more coordination and begin interacting with companions in the maternity groups. Gradually the juvenile baboons become independent although the continuing protection and guidance of the mother are essential even after gaining nutritional independence.

Young baboons as well as adults escape high predation levels probably because of the presence of adult males. Baboons respond to predators according to the developing situation. The distance of the predator to the troop in relation to the distance to the nearest cover plays a major role in the degree of anxiety that baboons show. Approaching water sources is thus a cautious exercise with adult males standing guard in trees or other vantage points. The bark of alarm is a conspicuous call that alerts members of the troop to move in the direction of the disturbance, identify it and assess the next step. Sometimes, adult males and females form a rearguard to protect the younger members of the troop upon the approach of a predator. On several occasions I saw lions kill baboons. Although it seems that lions do not particularly enjoy baboon meat as the carcasses were left almost intact, the baboons were killed swiftly at night because they presented too good an opportunity to miss.

Banded mongoose

Like the dwarf mongoose, the banded mongoose associates with wooded savannas and lives in the burrows in termite mounds. The banded mongoose is larger than the dwarf mongoose and eats insects and prey such as mice, toads, birds nesting on the ground and their eggs as well as lizards and snakes. They live in packs that include a number of breeding pairs. Rank seems to be determined by age and individual traits like boldness. The males engage more in the maintenance of territory boundaries through scent marking and are more aggressive towards members of neighboring packs than females. The turnover rate in pack members is low, although some of the packs may split if they reach a certain size.

The cohesion of mongoose groups is high and maintained through mutual scent marking and grooming. Like other members of the mongoose family, the banded mongoose relies much on the olfactory sense and marks objects as well as other members of its pack. The frequency and intensity of marking is a reflection of the degree of excitement. Pack members may take turns rubbing their cheeks and throats on particular objects or their own faeces and will generally adorn themselves with a communal and strong odor. This activity serves to provide a mutual identity and enhance confidence among pack members when confronting another pack or a predator. Meetings with other packs are infrequent, because home ranges

Banded mongoose are socialized creatures that forage in large groups.

Opposite:
Without the care of its mother the baby baboon is helpless. "Family support" is essential for the young's survival.

do not tend to overlap. Upon the sight of a neighboring pack, the packs tend to retreat rather than face a confrontation. If an encounter between two packs takes place, the bigger pack normally chases the smaller one. Fights may ensue between packs of the same size.

Even if observed in a camp site, it is difficult to keep up with a foraging pack of banded mongoose. They travel fast, mostly in a column, and hurry whenever they have to cross open spaces. A senior female is usually the leader while the juveniles lag behind. The mongooses scratch up litter and leaves, turn over stones and dung, and use their front claws to dig and extract beetle larvae and millipedes that they detect. Upon catching a relatively large prey, the mongoose shakes the prey and rolls it over using its front paws to kill prey that can cause harm, such as scorpions, centipedes and big spiders. Food sharing is common as the pack forages jointly within a small area. Nonetheless, aggressive interactions may ensue following the refusal of subordinate mongooses to allow adults access to food.

Banded mongoose always take advantage of their numbers when confronting predators. They will even mob predators larger than themselves and can successfully deter most potential predators, such as jackals, eagles and the serval. Interestingly, banded mongooses will also mob harmless animals like large birds and antelopes without apparent reason. Upon the first sign of a threat, the pack quickly clusters with the adults on the periphery protecting the young in the middle. Mutual defense reaches the extent that attempts are made to rescue members of the pack who have been caught by a predator.

The cohesiveness of the group is also shown in their reproductive behavior. Most births occur during the rains and reproduction is synchronized in the pack. Several females come into estrus simultaneously and mate with several different males. The young are suckled communally and pack members share the activities of raising the young, freeing the female to do her own foraging. Males also participate in the nursing, and teaching the young to forage.

A bat-eared fox uses his ears as radar receivers to detect the sound of burrowing insects below the ground.

Bat-eared fox

A common resident in the Savuti Marsh and throughout southern African arid savanna areas, the bat-eared fox is noted for its huge ears. Other than the aardwolf, it is among the most insectivorous carnivores. The majority of its food is made up of harvester termites, beetles and grasshoppers, although the proportion of particular invertebrate species in its diet varies seasonally according to temporary abundance. As such, mice might constitute a higher proportion in the diet at times when insects are scarce, such as the dry season.

Bat-eared fox are seen in pairs or family groups. The pair is monogamous but does not keep a territory, and the overlap of home ranges explains the sight of large groups within a small area. Feeding on insects is a laborious and time-consuming way to fill a stomach, partly because harvester termites run for their holes as soon as they sense that a predator is nearby, and a fox can only consume a limited number before the rest disappears. Its large ears and digging ability enable the fox to locate and recover beetle larvae and other subterranean invertebrates very efficiently. A searching fox moves in a random manner, turning its head from one side to the other, and cocking its ears in the hope of picking up the sounds that insects make when they move under the ground surface. Upon hearing a sound, the fox zooms in on the exact location of the prey by moving its ears like radar antennas, getting a fix on the location. Having effectively done so, the fox approaches and stands with its ears cupped above the spot where the prey is and begins digging, pausing ever so often to listen.

Tsessebe

A creature of grassland habitats, the tsessebe is the southern African population equivalent of the topi of East Africa. Its favorite grass species are mainly medium to tall grasses that grow in lightly wooded savannas. Its long, narrow muzzle and mobile lips are adapted for the selective feeding of young grass blades, avoiding mature and coarse leaves. However, the tsessebe is unable to mow short grass in the same way as bulk feeders such as wildebeest and zebra. Tsessebes are common in Savuti and on the fringes of the Okavango Delta all year round, as during the dry season they manage to subsist on water that the grasses provide.

The social organization of tsessebe appears to be more variable than any other antelope. In sedentary populations, males have large territories, whereas migratory populations have temporary and small territories in the aggregations. In resident populations, males may have an exclusive harem. Females take an active part in preventing foreign females and males from gaining access to the territory. Unlike many other antelopes such as impala and kudu, sexual dimorphism is non-existent and females may deceive intruders by acting as a male and adopting postures and performing territorial displays.

The maternal bond lasts until the mother gives birth to a new calf, when the first calf is a year old. Most yearling males join bachelor herds by the end of the calving season. These herds may include yearling females as they are also evicted by territorial males. Well-fed females may breed by the age of a year and a

Unlike their East African counterpart, tsessebe in southern Africa seldom use termite mounds as observation posts.

Albino animals like this kudu are rare in the wild, not only because of the low frequency of albino births, but also because albino animals are easily singled out by predators.

Opposite:
Among the predators of antelope are lions and other big carnivores. This hungry lion grimaces in anticipation of the hunt.

half, although males mature only in their third year, establishing territories later depending on population density and the prevailing sex ratio. Territorial displays in the forms of gland marking, ground horning and mud packing are performed by both sexes, although the frequency and the vigor of these displays are much greater with the territorial male.

Although the tsessebe is a medium-sized antelope which is a suitable prey size for most large predators on the African savanna, predation on adults is relatively light. This is probably because of its high level of alertness and speed by comparison to other antelopes of a similar size. Calves, however, are highly susceptible to predation, not only by large predators, but also by smaller ones, such as jackals. Breeding synchronization helps to increase the survival chances of individual calves. Tsessebe sometimes still hide their calves although they spend much of the time grazing in the open plains and may also be mobile. The calves rely on their camouflage and remain motionless lying close to the ground upon the approach of a predator. The females may leave the calves in hiding places and isolate them from the herd. Some females may even leave the herd's range to give birth and guard the calf during the early stages of growth.

Puku

The flood plains of the Chobe River mark the southernmost distribution range of the puku. The puku is associated throughout its distribution range with water, dwelling on grasslands at the edge of major waterways. Similar to the lechwe, puku utilize the stretches of soft green grass that lie between rivers and swamps and woodlands. They are predominantly grazers, feeding on various species of medium to tall grass. The proportion of each grass species in the diet of puku varies seasonally as well as annually, in relation to the local abundance of the species.

Puku occur in small herds that fluctuate in numbers as individuals come and go. Males are territorial although the defense of territories is predominantly through ritual displays and fighting is rare. Horn clashing may ensue upon the approach of a foreign male, although a territorial male may allow sub-adult males that are sexually inactive to enter his territory. There is no conspicuous breeding peak and calves are born at any time through the year. Calves are concealed soon after birth and do not have a strong instinct to follow their mother like, for example, the wildebeest. Upon the approach of predators, a calf may run in the opposite direction to its mother, who

Tsessebe gather at dusk at one of their feeding sites.

The Puku is the southern African relative of the Kob found in the flood plains of the Chobe River in northern Botswana.

Bottom, right:
A female kudu eats the salt that crusts on the surface of a mud pool. The salt supplements the kudu's otherwise poor diet with essential minerals, such as calcium and potassium.

does not make an effort to defend her calf. Nonetheless, the predation rate on puku by large predators seems to be relatively low due to the open habitat type that they choose to avoid ambushing. Furthermore, being a semi-aquatic species is advantageous against predators that are slow across flooded areas.

Sable antelope

One of the most gracious antelope species in Africa, the sable is unfortunately a rare species in many parts of its distribution range in Africa. It is restricted to southern African savannas and favors combinations of grasslands and woodlands. Similar to other selective feeders, it feeds entirely on grasses during the wet season. As the dry season progresses, it includes a high variety of plants in its diet including forbs and some browse. The movements of sable herds during this season are largely determined by the proximity of water sources and adjacent pastures. Sable are attracted to the flush of green grass growth that follows fires, as the quality of such forage is high, although with the lack of subsequent rains, the endurance of growth is short-lived. The sable is also known for visiting salt licks and frequenting termite mounds where both the grasses and the soils are enriched with minerals, particularly in areas with highly washed and porous soils.

An adult male sable parades with zebra on the way to a waterhole.

Opposite:
Reedbucks are found close to thick vegetation on the bank of rivers and flood plains.

Sable are found in herds, although large herds during the dry season usually constitute several small groups that disperse after the onset of the rains. Females establish a closed hierarchical society and avoid engagement with neighboring herds, except in the height of the dry season when the animals are obliged to subsist on limited resources that are concentrated in particular localities. Females normally stay in their natal home range. It seems that the knowledge of the home range is passed from one generation to the following and that descendants occupy the same home range indefinitely unless disturbed by humans. The top-ranking female in a herd is also the leader and the most vigilant member of the herd.

The dark and handsome sable males establish territories and spend much of the time by themselves. Bulls patrol the boundaries of their territories, typically along tracks, making frequent stops to sniff the ground for the dung and urine of other sable antelope. Males frequently trash bushes and young tree seedlings, and, as a result, the black horns of the sable may look brown because of the accumulation of bark between ridges on the horns. Bulls may retreat to thick bush during inactive periods, in stark contrast to their obtrusive behavior whenever they are with other sables. If a female herd enters the territory of a bull,

the bull will guard the rear of the herd, without trying to manipulate the direction of the herd. However, once they approach the boundary of the territory, the bull will try to dictate the direction of the herd. In fact, the territorial system of the sable antelope is unusual in the sense that dominant bulls are not confined to their own territories. Subordinate bulls that also establish territories tolerate the intrusion of dominant bulls, even if a female herd is present within their territory.

Sable typically reproduce at the height of the rainy season. The cows usually seek a hiding place before calving and remain alone with the calf for several weeks. Calves seek their mothers only to suckle, and the maternal bond is, in fact, so loose that calves may separate from their mothers within the sub-groups of a herd for several days. Juvenile males are harassed by the territorial bull when they reach around one and a half years of age, although they may stay in the herd until the age of four. By that time, the size and length of their horns stand out in comparison to mature females.

The proximity of the two impala males is indicative that the photograph was not taken during the rut season.

Right:
Stretching is a relaxing exercise for this juvenile impala.

During the rut, impala rams grunt and roar in an attempt to attract females and persuade them to stay as long as possible in the territory.

Left:
While drinking at the water-hole, vigilance is at its earnest.

Following pages:
Camel thorn trees dominate the sand ridges which mark the boundaries of old lakes.

A lion watches my vehicle with increasing impatience. I moved the vehicle soon after.

Right:
A lion at full charge.

Never taking his eyes from me, a lion continues to drink at a small pan in Chobe.

Left:
A lioness blends into the vegetation as it stalks prey.

285

Savuti is a good location to observe encounters between lions and elephants in the vicinity of the waterhole.

Elephants

Elephant ecology

Woodlands are quite a common vegetation form in semi-arid savannas. Elephants, together with fire, flooding regimes, soil properties, large herbivores and disease, play an extremely important part in regulating the densities of trees in savanna habitats. The objective of my research project was to investigate the question of how many elephants northern Botswana could, all in all, sustain. As such, it was a project based on the very dynamics of interactions between elephants and woodlands. Official estimates indicated that there were approximately 70,000 elephants wandering across 130,000 square kilometers in northern Botswana, with the majority of the population found on the northeastern periphery of the Okavango Delta. Elephants not only manage to endure the seasonal changes that entail a long, dry season, but also very much thrive under the conditions of the diverse habi-

tat types found throughout the region. The elephant population has been protected from ivory hunters since the time of the British administration (Bechuanaland Protectorate). A variety of surveys conducted by local biologists and independent researchers suggested that the increase of the elephant population in Botswana was due to a high calving rate, low poaching pressure, and immigration from neighboring countries where elephants are still persecuted. Some reports cautioned against the threat of allowing elephant numbers to increase beyond the carrying capacity of the land. Indeed, areas in the vicinity of permanent water sources, such as Chobe, Linyanti of Chobe National Park and Khwai in the Moremi Game Reserve, sustained heavy damage to mature woodlands and there was considerable concern that elephant concentrations along the riverine areas during the hot period of the dry season would ultimately change pristine riverine woodlands into ghost wastelands dominated by grasses and low scrub.

Elephant damage to vegetation is most prominent to the untrained eye at the height of the dry season.

Elephants are agents of habitat change. A single elephant consumes some 250 kilograms of vegetation daily, including grass, forbs, tree leaves and bark, fruits and pods. Elephant damage to the vegetation is particularly noticeable during the dry season when elephants concentrate on browse material that hold more nutrients than the dry and moribund grasses. Many woody plants also store nutrients in their bark. Elephants use their tusks to penetrate and peel the bark away from a tree. As a result, the supply of nutrients to the upper branches is depleted and the core becomes exposed to wood-burrowing insects and bacteria. Subsequently, the tree may die. Elephant herds also open thick scrub as they move through, breaking branches and trampling saplings. Elephant bulls are known for their "wasteful" eating habits as they tend to push down grown trees and nibble only some of the twigs before moving on. Presumably, the bulls test their strength against the sturdy tree trunks. Inevitably, the absolute food consumption capacity and the effects of elephant activities intensify their influence on the ecological balance in conservation areas where they are particularly abundant.

The elephant trunk

An elephant's trunk is an extension of its upper lip and nose. The trunk does not contain any bones and comprises thousands of muscles that enable it to perform complex and delicate tasks. The trunk can be extended to the ground and the elephant can feed from the ground level. When feeding on shrubs and trees, elephants typically grip branches at their base with their trunk and break them. This type of feeding leaves characteristic signs on the plants that can be easily identified. When I recorded the extent of damage to plants in northern Botswana, I was able to distinguish the signs that elephant trunks left on trees and shrubs and assess the extent of elephant damage to plants in relation to other types of damage, such as that caused by giraffes, disease, fire and wind.

The elephant bull on the left shakes a camel thorn tree for the pods, while his companions patiently wait for the pods to drop on the ground.

Mopane trees, a favorite elephant food, is resilient to their impact. Here a tree recovers after sustaining elephant damage that would kill other tree species.

Opposite:
Mud baths are a daily ritual for elephants when water is available.

The positioning of new artificial waterholes in national parks is a debatable subject because of the impact of wildlife on the vegetation in the vicinity of the site. Evidence suggests that in northern Botswana, the advantage of a waterhole as a tourist attraction may outweigh the localized damage to vegetation.

Though powerful enough to lift trees, the trunk is also a sensitive organ of smell and touch. Smell plays an important role in social contacts within a herd and in detecting water sources and potential enemies. The trunk also presents at its tips finger-like lips with fine sensory hairs. These lips enable the elephant to lift even quite small objects. In Chobe, the most common use of the lips is when elephants feed on the camel thorn acacia. When acacia pods mature, elephants, mostly bulls, move from one tree to the next. Whenever they reach a tree, they probe for pods on the branches and then shake the tree. Ripe pods fall to the ground and are picked up one by one from the ground using the trunk.

Further uses of the trunk include drinking, greeting, caressing and threatening, squirting water and throwing dust over its owner, and forming a range of vocalizations. Elephants drink by sucking water into their trunks, then squirting it into their mouths. Elephants also squirt water over their bodies and ears to cool themselves. The trunk can also serve as a snorkel whenever the elephants are submerged. Elephant calves have to learn the practicalities of using their trunk as they are not born with this knowledge. To human observers, one of the most humorous aspect of elephant behavior is watching baby elephants treating their trunks as extended rubber hoses.

Elephant behavior

Elephants are probably the highlight of the African experience for visitors who travel through the Chobe National Park. While elephants can be encountered almost anywhere in northern Botswana, elephant viewing along the Chobe riverine area is undeniably the most spectacular. Hundreds of elephants make their way from the woodlands in the south to the edge of the river under clouds of dust. The frequency of visits and length of journey to water sources vary considerably according to the prevailing weather conditions and the availability and quality of edible plants. The herds are comprised of family groups and one cannot remain indifferent seeing the cows tending their young while other calves play and explore the wonders of their trunks. If you watch elephants long enough, you will soon find that the family groups are very cohesive. Amazingly, the relationships between different groups do not correspond with our general perception of elephants as peaceful creatures. Periodically, a loud scream or a quick dash back to the safety of the herd will mark a family dispute and the development of a pecking order.

The principal social organization of elephants is a breeding herd dominated by a matriarch. This type of herd is typically called a family unit. The members of the unit consist of a mother with young and grown daughters with their offspring. Larger associations of elephants can also be found, particularly in the vicinity of water sources and preferred feeding sites. These associations comprise of family units and groups of mature bulls called bachelor herds. The matriarch determines the activity of the family unit. When the matriarch starts feeding, the herd spreads out and forages for food. When she starts moving, feeding stops and all the individuals join her. Upon the slightest hint of disturbance, members of the family group cluster together around the matriarch and follow her lead. Leadership and experience play a prominent role in the elephant society. Typically, the most experienced female becomes the matriarch, and she will continue to lead the herd well beyond the age of

The trunk is stretched forward to absorb as much information as possible. In this case, an elephant investigates the cause of death of a fellow elephant.

Opposite:
An elephant cow carefully guides her calf in the search for undigested food items buried in fresh dung.

reproduction. The sudden loss of the matriarch, commonly as a result of shooting, disrupts and confuses the members of the herd. They mill around or stay close to their struck leader, exposing themselves to poacher's bullets. Members of a herd will try to support and attempt to raise a wounded companion, and elephants will support injured and handicapped members for several days, until the diminishing supply of food and water in the vicinity will force them to abandon the wounded elephant. A matriarch who becomes too feeble to lead the herd either leaves or is abandoned by her family. The next oldest cow then takes the leadership of the herd.

Leadership is also determined according to individual characteristics. Thus, it is not imperative that age seniority gives an automatic admission for herd leadership. The measure of aggressiveness and assertiveness among mature cows plays an important role in the determination of the appropriate successor.

Old and solitary elephants may spend their last days in the vicinity of water courses where the lush green vegetation and the ample supply of water provide temporary refuge. Hence, the occasional appearance of unusually high numbers of elephant carcasses along permanent river courses. This may also be the source of folk stories describing graveyards of elephants that are stocked with ivory.

Photographing young calves is a difficult task when encountering wild elephant herds. The mothers are very protective of the calves, hiding them underneath, or putting themselves between the photographer (who is regarded as a potential threat) and the calf.

Family members are frequently seen touching each other with their trunks while resting or drinking. They lean and rub their bodies against each other as well. Elephants greet each other by inserting their trunks into the mouth of the other, with the elephant that inserts the trunk tip considered subordinate. It is a gesture of peace and neutralizes aggression between members of different groups. This behavior pattern may originate from the calves' habits of putting their trunks into their mothers' mouth to sample food and

Opposite:
Unlike their East African counterparts, the tusks of the southern African elephants are relatively small. Hence, exceptions are always striking.

Below:
Although elephants are annoyed by the close proximity of lions, they become quite inquisitive if they sense that the intention of lions is not hostile.

A young elephant calf already articulates a threat display through flapping its ears.

also receive reassurance. The trunk may also be extended to approaching elephants or even adversaries. There is a difference, though, in the degree the trunk is extended towards each of the objects. When elephants extend trunks towards companions, it is a greeting sign and serves to signal friendly intentions. Extending trunks towards adversaries is seen on rare occasions and probably gives the elephant a better opportunity to receive olfactory information.

Elephants drink some 150 liters of water daily. Nonetheless, they can withstand several days without drinking and can venture up to 80 kilometers away from water sources. Elephants in the Kaokoveld in Namibia are particularly known for their long endurance. These elephants, however, do not differ from elephants in savanna areas. There is a significant difference between mature bulls and cows in the sense that bulls tend to cover larger distances in their search for water and food. The reason for this discrepancy might be related to the presence of calves in breeding

herds that limits the time and distance that can be traveled without water. Hence the abundance of bulls in areas far from permanent water sources during the height of the dry season. Bulls may also satisfy their thirst by digging in the sand of dry river beds. With their acute sense of smell, elephants detect moisture from a distance and will dig in places where the water table is high. Digging is performed using the tusks, trunk and the legs to remove excess soil. The hole is then enlarged with the trunk and may reach the depth of three meters.

Elephants love water. They roll and wallow in shallows and may submerge completely in deep water. The sight of elephants swimming in the Chobe River is a common one. At certain points, the level of water is high and forces the elephants to swim. They swim very much like dogs do, and learn to swim at an early age when shallow rivers pose a formidable obstacle. After overcoming their fear of entering the water, calves rest the tips of their trunks on the hindquarters

of their mothers, assuring a continuous supply of air through the nostrils. After crossing, the mothers assist the calves that struggle to clumb up the slippery banks by pulling the calves with their trunks.

At small waterholes, elephants use their trunks to hose themselves with water. After slaking their thirst, elephants use their trunks to splatter themselves with mud. Self-dusting may follow, usually accompanied also with rubbing against objects available in the vicinity, such as thick tree trunks and round termite mounds. Elephants are very meticulous with their mud and dust splattering. It is believed that the purpose of this behavior is two-fold – firstly, as relief from parasites such as ticks that infest folds in the skin where the trunk cannot reach, and secondly as a thermo-regulatory device. By adding a coat of wet mud, elephants enjoy some relief from the heat.

Male elephants leave the maternal herd when they reach adolescence (about 12 to 13 years of age). A mature bull is never found for a long period among a breeding herd. The separation of the young bulls from the herd is a gradual process. Adolescent bulls show signs of maturity when they try to mount or harass females. The females become intolerant of this sexually precocious behavior and the matriarch will push them to the periphery of the herd where they remain and satellite the family unit at a distance. Having become independent, the young bulls associate with other bulls, or may wander alone. Immature bulls tend to associate with their peers while mature bulls tend to venture alone. During periods of musth, the rut of elephants, bulls wander over extensive areas and leave their bachelor group in a search for mating opportunities.

Antagonistic Behaviour in Elephants

Elephants are the largest land mammals. As such, they are, perhaps, the true rulers of the jungle (and savanna for that matter). Size is an important – if not the most important – factor that determines the outcome of conflicts over food sources, territory and mating rights. Although elephants appear for most of the time quiet and complacent, they can present a very complex set of antagonistic postures and movements to express escalating levels of aggression. Spreading the ears and holding them in a forward position or flapping them is a sign of mounting tension. To observers coming closer to elephants on foot or in a vehicle, elephants spreading their ears are signalling, "be careful, we are aware that you are approaching." Elephants also spread their ears and flap them to regulate their temperature, or simply to hear better. However, it is

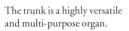

The trunk is a highly versatile and multi-purpose organ.

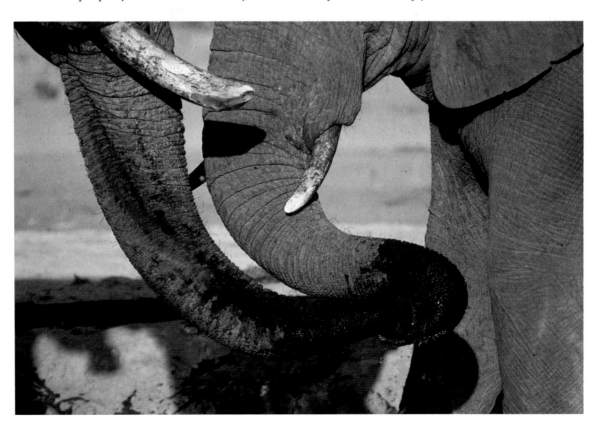

easy for the human observer to distinguish between these situations.

Elephants use a complex body language to express their intentions. An angry elephant may raise or extend its trunk. A raised tail also serves to indicate aggression or fear. Normally, few members of the herd will respond to such movements. However, if these movements are accompanied by the elephant lifting his head high, other elephants nearby take immediate note. A frightened elephant will retreat, walking with a peculiar high gait, its tail held high and ears erect.

Predictably, elephants will avoid confrontation for the risk of injury. Yet, if they feel cornered or the lives of their calves are threatened, mothers will not hesitate to attack in order to kill. For the purpose of avoiding a conflict when danger is not imminent, there are levels of aggression which can be expressed to deter a potential enemy or to warn an adversary. Walking toward an adversary while nodding the head with ears half spread is a common display between cows. Merely turning toward a potential antagonist is also a mild threat that serves to reinforce dominance in the herd. A threatened individual generally gives way without responding. Jerking the head in a single abrupt upward movement, followed by a slow return, is another sign, while head tossing is a more pronounced version. The head is lowered and then lifted sharply so that the tusks perform an arc. A more aggressive movement is head shaking. The head first twists to one side, and then quickly rotates to the other side, causing the ears to slap and dust to blow, and making quite an impressive noise.

Trumpeting accompanies a movement of the trunk forward. This threat is normally performed towards a smaller adversary. The trunk is rolled up, then abruptly swished towards the opponent. For emphasis, elephants might pick grass, dust or branches and throw the objects toward the opponent. Although I had such an experience, I never witnessed elephants throwing objects at other elephants.

If all warnings fail and the enemy, most commonly people, ignore the signs and continue to approach the elephant, they will attack. There are two distinct types of attacks. The mock attack feigns a true attack but the elephant has no intention to come in contact with the enemy. Signs of indecision are normally evident and confirm that the elephant is not prepared to press home the attack. In my experience, these signs are very subtle and not always evident. Contrary to the common belief, the position of the trunk is not an indication of the intention of the elephant. The trunk is a very sensitive organ and elephants fold their trunk backwards when attacking. However, in an attack they may extend the trunk forward, or leave it loose until the last moment. The distance of the attack is perhaps the best indication of the intention. Angry elephants that are determined to press home their attack charge from a far distance. The observer may seldom be aware of the attacker until the elephant is very close. In an attack, elephants are silent until they come into contact with the enemy. At that point, they trumpet, probably to express and reinforce their aggressive intention. In a mock attack, the elephant will stop short of the enemy and throw dust and branches and stand high. Then, in a sudden movement, the elephant will retreat with its tail held high and look for an object nearby to displace its anger. Bushes are favorite victims because they can be trashed easily and make an impression on the enemy.

The elephant attack

Nogatssa is a tourist camp site situated in the heart of the Chobe National Park. The camp is not frequented by tourists because it is located a long way inland at the end of a bumpy track. It is, however, a rendezvous point for herds of elephants on their annual migration towards the northern water courses. Hence, the diversity of habitat types and the abundance of elephants make the site an ideal study area.

During one of my visits to Nogatssa, I had Earthwatch volunteers with me. On a previous visit, we had the camp site and the nearby water trough for ourselves. There were very few animals in the area and elephants were not seen. A month later, the whole area was teeming with elephant herds. The annual migration north had begun. The water supplied by a solar powered pump was just keeping up with the demand of the thirsty elephants. I explored the trough to find that elephants had fouled the water and it had become a mud bath. I then looked for an alternative source and headed along the route of an underground pipe that fed water from the pump to the trough. Elephants standing near the trough showed no signs of stress, and were standing idly around the waterhole, occasionally drinking from a trough which funneled water into a large reservoir. The serene atmosphere was interrupted by the sound of water gushing inside the elephants' trunks and down their throats, mingled with the continual cooing drift of doves.

The ten Earthwatch research assistants were admiring the majestic sight of herds walking silently to the water's edge, satisfying their thirst, and fading into the thick brush. I, however, was too preoccupied with logistics to appreciate the remarkable spectacle

Elephant bulls may opt not to wander to permanent water sources in the north but supplement their water requirements by digging in the dry river beds.

Elephants love water. An
elephant bull plays in a pan in
the Chobe National Park.

Right:
An afternoon bath by the banks
of the Chobe River.

An elephant bull solicits his mate to take a dip in the cool water of a pan.

Left:
Elephants play in the Chobe River.

Savuti is a place frequented by
elephant bulls. Some elephants
became very tolerant to the
presence of humans.

offered by the largest remaining elephant herd in Africa. The water that we had brought over was not sufficient for us to stay long enough to complete the fieldwork, and we had to rely on the water supply from the pump that was feeding the trough. The pump was situated within short walking distance of the camp. Across the waterhole not far away from our newly erected camp there was a mixed herd of elephants comprised of bulls, cows and some juveniles standing by a dead acacia tree.

As I was walking towards the pump, I came closer to the elephant herd. Some of them had their ears raised already, indicating that they were alerted to my presence some 60 meters away. I noticed that there were no infants in the group. Presumably, the cows were rather unlikely to respond aggressively to my approach. I turned my gaze to the ground and closely followed the track of the pipe line while the elephants turned and moved parallel to my line of travel.

Suddenly, they spread out and veered, line abreast, closing the distance between us within few seconds. Instantly, I recognized that this was not a mock charge. I was tempted to retreat to the camp, but that would certainly have been fatal as elephants can accelerate to a speed of 30 kilometers an hour without effort, and would tackle me from behind. I began jumping and waving my arms in a futile attempt to look bigger and persuade the elephants to abandon their charge. Normally, this exercise works and ends with spectacular threat and displacement displays. Like many other animals, elephants are reluctant to attack unless they feel cornered. Their sheer size is also a factor that induces self-confidence and thus they are reluctant to charge without warning. However, on this occasion, I was confronted by a herd that was committed to a common decision, which was to kill me. There were two possible explanations for their behavior. These elephants may have been intimidated

Elephant bulls and lions meet at sunrise around the Savuti waterhole.

A matriarch covering the retreat of her family. Road crossing is a cause for anxiety among many animals that recognize the imprints of man.

Previous pages:
A moment of truth. A herd of elephants seriously charging.

in the past by poachers and resented the proximity of people. The elephants could also have been disturbed by me, but could not choose another exit route because other herds were obstructing their path.

By now two bulls were running ahead of the herd on the right side and I advanced towards the opposite flank to avoid them. There was no way out. I was confronted by an angry elephant who tossed me high up in the air using his forehead as he stormed along with the herd. For a split second, I got a bird's-eye view of the herd passing underneath me. I landed and rolled sideways to avoid other members of the herd. To my horror, the elephants turned around and came back charging. I yelled to the people at the camp to bring a vehicle, but my cries were drowned by the rage of the elephants. I was tossed up again by a cow. This time, I could anticipate what was coming and I managed to

avoid her legs and tusks altogether. After landing, I could not get up because the elephants were gathering around me. A sunny afternoon darkened under a veil of grey skins and a dusty barrage of elephant bodies. On the edges of the group, I had a glimpse of elephants kneeling down and plowing the ground with their tusks, in an attempt to impale me. I made a considerable effort to stay in center of the herd between the elephants and avoid being thrown outside. I was bounced between their legs that were like concrete pillars with the coarse mud crusts. I could hear nothing but the whisk of skins and deep rumbles. Some individuals, however, departed to the sanctuary of the bush, having realized that the threat was removed. More light penetrated through the dust cloud. Suddenly, I found myself on my back and underneath the belly of a large bull, who kneeled and managed to tusk

my right leg and tear my Achilles tendon. He tried again, but I withdrew my legs and the elephant's tusks and lower jaw hit the ground with a loud thud. Then, with the same suddenness of the attack, the elephant fled after the rest of the herd. I managed to pick myself up. I felt no pain. Pieces of skin and tendon were hanging loose from my lower leg but there was little bleeding. Through the grass stalks I could see the volunteers coming to my rescue.

Elephant management

Although young elephants are killed by lions and hyenas, the elephant's most dangerous enemy is man. Hunting for ivory was a common practice centuries ago and caused the extinction of elephants from large parts of their traditional home range in West and northern Africa, south of the Sahara. In addition, the spread of settlements, agriculture and pastoralism also brought about the permanent eviction of elephants from their preferred habitats. The introduction of technology, including firearms, accelerated the rate of decline of elephant populations. It is estimated that between the 1970s and the late 1980s, the African elephant population plummeted from one and a half million to approximately half a million elephants.

As their former habitats are destroyed and their numbers cut in the greed for ivory, the only hope for the future conservation of elephants lies in national parks and game reserves. Controlled and well-managed national parks protect elephants from poachers and provides suitable conditions for elephants to maintain their natural life cycle. However, the higher survival rates of calves brings about an increase in elephant numbers within a park. At the same time, human harassment from outside the boundaries drives elephants into the sanctuary of the park. Ultimately, the number of elephants are determined by the supply of food. Density-dependent mechanisms, such as delayed age of puberty, an increase in the interval between births, an earlier age of menopause and an increase in infant mortality are indicators that elephants have reached the capacity of food supply in the park. It is feared, however, that these mechanisms are slow and not always effectvie. As a result, high elephant densities may cause the decline of tall trees and shrubs irreversibly. This results in the conversion of the habitat from woodland to grassland.

Fears that national parks would be irreversibly damaged by elephants have caused fierce controversy since the late 1960s. Management-orientated conservationists claim that since the increase of elephant populations in national parks is a result of artificial intervention, humans should maintain control and cull excess numbers of elephant to maintain the natural balance within the parks and prevent the loss of plants and animals that dwell in habitats that the elephants alter. Other conservationists argue in favor of leaving nature to take its own course. Essentially, these conservationists claim that the increase in elephant populations is a phase in a natural cycle and that numbers will decline affording the regeneration of trees and the reestablishment of woodlands. Therefore, culling is not necessary to restore the natural balance.

My research project in Chobe was to probe the question of how many elephants the region could sustain. It was obvious that the survival of woodlands in northern Botswana not only depended on the impact of elephants, but also on the effects of other factors such as fire and disease. These factors may act in accord or separately on the woodlands. I found that elephants did not necessarily escalate the extent of damage to plants in addition to other factors. Furthermore, in northern Botswana the effects of elephants and fire on woodland habitats are largely fragmented. Data gathered from woodland habitats of the red Kalahari Sand plateau that covers an extensive part of northern Botswana showed that woodlands dominated by the Rhodesian Teak (*Baikiaea plurijuga*) were subjected to serious fire damage, most of which was caused by runaway fires ignited by pastoralists and hunters on the peripheries of the reserves. The purpose of burning is to propagate the growth of nutritious grass that attracts herbivores and nourishes livestock. Although many elephants roam in Rhodesian Teak woodlands, not enough elephant damage appeared on plants to suggest that elephants alter the woodland structure and prompt tree mortality. Conversely, woodlands dominated by mopane (*Colophospermum mopane*), which is a principal food item for elephants in the region, were dominated by elephant-induced damage that in turn influenced plant densities and overall vegetation structure, although some fire damage was also observed. Preliminary results aided by mathematical models described a certain threshold for elephants in different habitat types. While the current number of elephants could be well sustained by the vegetation, fire has a devastating effect on some woodland habitats. Thus, the control of fire should receive greater attention from the local Department of Wildlife to ensure the future welfare of woodlands. In other words, from an ecological perspective, there is no justification to cull elephants in order to maintain the natural balance in the park and surrounding areas.

Earthwatch Corps volunteers collecting data in the field.

Opposite, top:
Reliable results follow long and tedious hours of fieldwork.

Opposite, bottom:
The demise of eco-tourism. A Nile monitor is disorientated after getting his head stuck in a leftover can. After taking the photograph, I released the monitor from the can.

All the camp sites were open to wildlife to come and go as they pleased. Some camps were close to waterholes that elephants frequented.

Fieldwork

When I began my graduate studies and headed into the bush to conduct fieldwork, my supervisor, Professor John Skinner, Head of the Mammal Research Institute at the University of Pretoria gave me some guidelines for research. He indicated that for every hour in the field, one has to spend at least three hours at the university for the purpose of lab work, data analysis, literature research and writing down the results. Since my original intention was to stay in the bush rather than spend time at the university, I managed to more than reverse the rule. From the beginning, my interest encompassed the subject of animal behavior and ecology. Many researchers that specialize in these fields radio-collar animals so that they can closely follow the animals and gain as much information as possible about their behavioral patterns and the relationships between the animals and the environment. I stayed clear of any aspect related to radio-collaring. No matter how attractive and somewhat useful such technology might be, I felt that the time and effort required to locate and capture the animals, was not reflected in the quality of data derived. Instead, I dedicated much effort to the study of plants and soils that are the basic components of every terrestrial ecosystem. This orientation paid handsomely.

Since plants and soils do not move, are readily accessible and yield large quantities of data, I was free to manage my time in the field more efficiently.

All in all, I spent more time observing animals in the field and photographing them than I spent on data collection. It was most rewarding. Through observing the animals, I got to grips with the ways of wildlife without sacrificing the value of scientific work. Moreover, these aspects were complementary. Clearly, there was no use in gaining dry scientific data without knowing the animals, and vice versa. As I gained experience, I understood that each place has its own rhythm. The animals have their routine and daily and seasonal cycles that make the bush such a rich and vibrant environment. Without knowing the rhythms, the bush experience is like watching an erratic procession of animals and events. It takes time to understand and converge with the rhythms of life. Nonetheless, once you are in it, you become entirely immersed. I woke up with the animals and drove to where I could see cheetahs starting their daily hunt and birds clustering for their first drink. When activity subsided towards mid-morning through to the late afternoon, I was busy with the plants and soils. As the sun set its

course to the edge of the horizon, it was time for a resumed burst of activities, watching elephants attending their young and lions getting ready for the night hunts. Accurately anticipating events was the best indication of how well I knew the animals, and when animals surprised me with unexpected deviations from their routine, it was another reason to enjoy being amongst them.

During the course of research in northern Botswana, I had Earthwatch volunteers to assist me with the fieldwork. Earthwatch Corps is a non-profit company that sends volunteers to projects throughout the world led by qualified scientists in a wide range of fields. The volunteers pay their costs and the major contribution to the work of scientists is the provision of manpower for the collection of data. Although it sounds simple and convenient, delegating volunteers in the bush to sample plants was not an easy task. Nonetheless, the volunteers collected an ample amount of data that enhanced the databases that I had already acquired about the relationships between elephants and their habitats in the region. Whenever I ran an expedition, I used to take the volunteers to a site where I was measuring the extent of damage to plants by elephants and other factors, such as fire, disease and herbivores. Damage caused by elephants and fire was easy to recognize, and so were the plant species that I was concentrating on. Thus, there was no problem in assigning volunteers who had never

been in Africa and never seen an elephant in the wild to the routine of fieldwork. After a training session, the volunteers were grouped in pairs with each pair assigned to a stretch of bush. While sampling, volunteers measured the densities of plants of different height classes and assessed the extent of elephant and fire damage within small squares. The work was tedious, but most of the 200 volunteers that came did a fine job. In the end, priorities changed and having volunteers was no longer viable for the project.

Wildlife economics

Ever since the proclamation of Yellowstone, national parks have been established in many countries throughout the world. From a legal point of view, parks are the most secure haven for wilderness, protecting natural assets from the development pressures of the outside world. However, pressures are likely to grow and natural resources to dwindle with time. Several solutions have been proposed to maintain and enhance wildlife conservation in Africa. In essence, the proposals tie revenues generated in the parks with the welfare of the local people. Ideally, local communities will have strong incentives to safeguard their income sources, in other words, the adjoining nature reserves. Currently, neighboring communities exert most of the pressure on game reserves, through poaching, invasion with livestock, burning, agriculture practices and the use of pesticides. In addition, animals

Unless local communities become more actively involved in the conservation of land, malpractice such as over-stocking cattle may cause the decline of living standards and the destruction of natural ecosystems.

such as elephants and lions raid crops and kill live-stock. From the perspectives of local people, the nature reserves are potential land for development, and also a threat. Viable solutions cater for the economic involvement of local communities in the development of the tourist infrastructure of nature reserves. In reserves where tourist potential is low, it is possible for locals to utilize natural resources on a sustainable yield basis, such as timber, firewood, thatch grass as well as game meat and the supervision of professional hunters that hunt trophy animals.

Sustainable yield has become a buzz word for the utilization of natural resources. For example, managers of a game farm might plan to subsist (and profit) from the marketing of game meat from impala and kudu. Under the constraints of the size of the farm, there is only a certain number of impala and kudu that the reserve can carry. This term is called the carrying capacity. For each animal species, there is only a certain maximum number that can subsist on the available resources, namely grasses and browse mater-

ial. A surplus of that number disrupts the flow of natural cycles quite considerably. Animals start dying of hunger after over-exploiting the resources, and a severe crash in animal numbers will follow. The recovery of numbers to the former thresholds may take many years, to the extent that sometimes the animals do not manage to reach the full capacity because of permanent habitat destruction. In essence, this is the ecological balance which is much sought-after by scientists and managers of nature reserves. Knowledge of these natural limits enables managers to reach sound decisions about how many impalas and kudus they can crop without affecting the ecological balance, so that they can sustain their enterprise effectively.

The key to the future success of game reserves and national parks in Africa is the involvement of local communities in their operation and the chance to benefit from revenues that reserves generate.

Following pages:
The early morning sun illuminates a male leopard that found refuge in a tall tree after being chased by lions.

Epilogue

At the time I was injured in the elephant attack, I had been in Africa for almost a decade. This was a far cry from what I had dreamed of as a small boy, standing by the side of a tourist kombi watching a herd of elephants grazing peacefully in the woodland nearby. I clearly remember then wanting to stay forever. Of course, reality blurred my determination over the years. And by the time I was making enquires about graduate degrees in southern Africa, I could hardly imagine myself being immersed in the African bush. Nonetheless, once I reached the bush, the place where life was so vivid and vibrant, I settled there, gently, as if it was my natural home. Even now, when I no longer stay for long periods in the bush, the sights, sounds and smells remain with me. Yet when I go back there, it takes a while to grasp the rhythms of the bush. I suppose that this is what it means to become rusty. But the feelings remain the same, the sheer exuberance and happiness.

In my early days in the bush, I was very committed to taking photographs. I wanted to absorb everything and I found that taking photographs was the best means to achieve that goal. There was a price, however. When there were other people in a vehicle with me I resented their presence, particularly if they had their own camera equipment and when something dramatic was happening, such as a lion taking a kill, the vehicle would rock with the excitement of everyone on board and I was left with a collection of blurred photographs and a growing sense of frustration. Yet over the period of my time in Africa, I had plenty of opportunities to witness events that few people see. Gradually, my desire to take the ultimate photograph subsided. Instead, I felt that I wanted to share this unique experience because it was so

captivating. Nowadays, whenever I go on safari I take a backseat and enjoy the excitement of other people. Did I really look so anxious for the sight of an animal, not wanting to miss a thing? And those photographs that I missed are cemented like hanging images in my memory. I hope that this subtle tension of the African bush has been conveyed through the pages of this book. The best part, however, is that there is so much more than the photograph, or the eye, can ever see.

Me with an elephant herd near my base camp in the heart of the Chobe National Park.

Glossary

Adult: an individual that is both physically and reproductively mature.

Aestivation: a dormant period of escape from drought.

Alpha: the top ranking member of a dominance hierarchy order.

Altricial: an animal born helpless, often with eyes closed and with limited locomotion ability that requires its parents for constant care and protection, e.g. a monkey.

Aquatic: animals that live in fresh water.

Arboreal: animals that live in trees.

Arid zone: a region of low rainfall with rather sparse vegetation cover that acts as a link between desert and savanna areas.

Bachelor group: an all-male association.

Binocular vision: the visual field within the view of both eyes. Owls, cats and monkeys have eyes that have an overlap in vision for estimating depth.

Biota: the animals, plants, fungi, etc., of a particular region or period.

Browse: tender shoots or twigs of shrubs and trees as food for cattle, deer, etc. (browsers).

Bushveld: a stretch of uncultivated land covered with mixed plant growth, thick bush and other vegetation, trees, etc.

Calcrete pan: soil sediments, permeated with calcium salts, forming a hard pan that holds rain water.

Carnivore: a mammal belonging to the order Carnivora, such as dogs, cats, lions, wild dogs, mongoose and hyena. Most carnivores, however, also eat food other than meat.

Carrion: dead and putrefying flesh.

Colony: a group of organisms of the same kind living or growing in close association.

Cud: a bolus of partially digested vegetation that a ruminant regurgitates, chews, insalivates and swallows again while ruminating.

Deciduous: 1. shedding the leaves annually, as certain trees and shrubs; 2. falling off or shed at a particular season, stage of growth, etc., as leaves, horns, or teeth.

Desert: a region where rainfall is sporadic. Normal annual rainfall is less than 150mm per year.

Dispersion pattern: the characteristic grouping pattern of a species or a population of animals.

Displacement activity: a behavior that is displaced from its original or normal context. Feeding and grooming behavior patterns are often performed during aggressive interactions with other individuals to displace anger, stress and frustration. For example, an elephant that threatens an enemy displaces its anger by ripping a nearby bush to pieces.

Display: a behavioral pattern that has been modified in the course of evolution to a ritual in order to transmit a specific kind of information to a receiver.

Diurnal: active by day, as certain birds and insects (opposed to nocturnal).

Dung midden: the pile of dung or droppings that accumulate through regular deposits. A midden often marks the boundary of a territory and corresponds with scent reception as opposed to the visual cues of the pile.

Ecological niche: a particular set of adaptations that modifies a species to specific environmental conditions and vary from the requirements of other species.

Ecosystem: a community of organisms together with the physical environment in which they live.

Ecotone: the transitional zone between different habitat types.

Endemic: native plants and animals that are found only in specific localities and not elsewhere.

Estivate: the equivalent of hibernating in a warm climate.

Estrus: a behavior pattern associated with ovulation. Most mammalian females are sexually receptive only at that period.

Forage: 1. food for animals, especially when taken by browsing or grazing; 2. the act of foraging: search for provisions.

Forbs: herbs other than grasses that are common in grasslands and may have conspicuous flowers.

Grazer: a herbivore that eats mainly grasses.

Harem: a group of two or more females that are owned by a male.

Hemotoxic: a substance contained in snake venom which perforates the blood vessels and causes hemorrhage.

Herbivore: an animal whose diet solely consists of plant food.

Herd: a social group of animals consisting of at least two adults of the same sex. The term generally applies to gregarious ungulates.

Hierarchy: a rank order applied to social groups in which a high ranking member dominates most others except for individuals of higher ranks.

Home range: the area occupied by an individual or a group as defined by the occurrence of the animals in a given area within a certain period.

Insectivorous: an animal whose diet consists primarily of insects.

Invertebrate: any animal without a spinal column; diverse category, ranging from microscopic protozoans to giant squids.

Juvenile: the stage between infancy and adolescence.

Kilometer: 1 km equals 0.6214 miles.

Lek: a breeding ground or arena where territorial males cluster around a central location, to which estrus females come to mate with the most centrally situated males. Males compete for the locations and it is expected that the fittest males establish the most centrally situated locations.

Mammals: any vertebrate of the class Mammalia; their bodies are more or less covered with hair, they are warm-blooded, nourish their young with milk from the mammary glands, and, with few exceptions, give birth to live young.
Meter: 1 m equals 3.2808 feet.
Migration: movement from one region to another where conditions are better, often in response to seasonal changes.
Mobbing: cooperative attack by members of a group, triggered by behavior of the attacked animal or by a signal from the group members. Mobbing also refers to the harassment by a single individual of a nearby potential predator.
Monogamy: A mating system in which most individuals have only one sexual partner. Often, the duration of association between a pair is for life.
Musth: term for elephants in heat or estrus.

Nocturnal: animals that are primarily night active.

Olfactory: organs and traits related to the sense of smell.
Omnivore: an animal that feeds both on plant and animal material.
Organic substrate: the organic level of soil in which plants grow.

Pasting: hyenas marking their territory by secreting a sticky white paste from their anal glands.
Polygamy: a mating system of species with more than one partner.
Precocial: animals that are born well developed with eyes open and a full locomotion ability, e.g. a chick.
Predator: an animal that subsists mainly on eating live prey, usually vertebrates rather than invertebrates.
Preorbital: in front of each eye, where a gland appears in some ungulate species.
Primate: member of the mammalian order Primates, which includes humans, apes, monkeys, and prosimians, or lower primates.
Pronking: a distinctive bounding gait in which the animal bounces off the ground with stiff and straight legs, mostly performed by medium-sized antelopes when alarmed.

Raptor: a raptorial bird.
Ruminant an ungulate with a four-chambered stomach, which chews the cud as part of the rumination process.
Rut: a mating period during which most conceptions occur. A rut may be indicated by males displaying to attract females and establish territories.

Savanna: a landscape form typical of tropical zones in which the ground layer is dominated by grasses with interspersed trees. The distribution of rainfall and densities and composition of tree species in savanna areas are the keys for the various definitions of savanna types. Accordingly, wet savanna with deciduous trees have rainfall above 500mm per year. Semi-arid savannas commonly have sparse tree cover that receive less than 500mm rainfall per year.
Scavenger: an animal or other organism that feeds on dead organic matter.
Sedentary population: the inactive or non-migratory inhabitants of an area.
Sexual dimorphism: differences in form between males and females, usually resulting from the development of male characters in response to sexual selection pressures, such as larger size, horns and large tusks.
Species: a population, or several populations of closely related and similar organisms that are capable of inbreeding freely and do not produce any offspring or viable offspring if mating takes place with organisms of a different species.
Spoor: a track or trail, esp. that of a wild animal pursued as game; from Africaans "footprint."
Sub-adult: close to adult age.
Succulent: 1. (of a plant) having fleshy and juicy tissues; a succulent plant, as a sedum or cactus.
Symbiotic: a mutually dependent relationship between unrelated organisms that are intimately associated e.g. bacteria in the rumen of ruminants and wasps in the fruit of sycamore fig.

Territorial: animals that defend a particular area against rivals of the same species.
Translocation: 1. a change of location; 2. *Bot.* the conduction of soluble food material from one part of a plant to another.

Ungulate: a mammal with hooves.

Veld: an Afrikaans term for field, generally used in southern Africa to describe savanna areas.
Vomeronasal organ: (also known as Jacobson's organ) a pair of narrow and blind sacs situated on either side of the nasal crevices lined with sensory cells. The system is present in many mammal species and is mostly dedicated to monitor the reproductive condition of females.

Index

Index

Z A I R E
A N G O L A
Benguela
Oshakati
Livingstone
Maun
N A M I B I A
B O T S W A N A
Windhoek
Gaboron
Johannesburg
Lüderitz
A T L A N T I C O C E A N
R E P U B L I C O F
S O U T H A F R I C A
Cape Town